ORAL INTERPRETATION OF BIBLICAL LITERATURE

by

Chloe Armstrong

Department of Oral Communication

Baylor University

Waco, Texas

Burgess Publishing Company

426 South Sixth Street • Minneapolis, Minn. 55415

PREFACE

The awareness of the need for ministers, religious leaders and laymen who can read the Bible aloud effectively has motivated the writing of this book.

It would be presumptuous of me to state too explicitly where and how this book can be used. However, it is intended for a supplementary textbook in classes of oral interpretation, literature, and religion, for church groups, and for those who would like to develop a greater appreciation and understanding of the Scriptures through oral reading.

Oral Interpretation of Biblical Literature is based on two concepts: the Bible is literature and was written to be read aloud; the oral interpreter of the Bible must have the ability to understand the Scriptures and the skill to communicate this understanding to his audience.

This volume deals primarily with suggestions and methods of procedure in the study of the literature of the Bible and suggestions and techniques for development of skill of oral reading. Throughout the chapters I have offered suggestions rather general in nature but specific enough to be helpful to the reader. But I have not attempted to formulate a set of exact rules.

I am indebted to many people for their help and encouragement in writing this book. I would acknowledge in particular Glenn Capp, Chairman of the Oral Communication Department, Baylor University, for his aid and counsel and James Wood, Professor of Religion, Baylor University, for his suggestions and guidance in preparing the manuscript.

Chloe Armstrong

September, 1968

CONTENTS

Dedicated to

The Memory of

My Mother and Father

Chapter One

WHY READ THE BIBLE ALOUD

Most people will agree with Bishop Horace W. B. Danegan when he says: "It is essential that people should read the Bible itself. But it is equally important that they should know how to read it."[1] Oral interpretation offers one approach to *know how to read* scripture.

The Oral Tradition of the Bible

Oral reading places the Bible in its natural habitat. It was intended to be read aloud. Long before anyone in Israel thought of writing in literary form, people told stories, listened to wise sayings and riddles, and handed them down from generation to generation in the oral tradition. Much of Biblical history is traditional and relies upon the oral tradition of handing down narratives and recording events and sayings from the past. The historical and biographical portions of the Bible were told and retold and circulated from country to country long before they were written down. The early prophets delivered their messages orally; they were not concerned with writing down their pronouncements. It was left for others to gather together the messages and to record them retaining for the most part the oral style of the prophet. The prophet Isaiah, when the people seemed to avoid the prophecy of woe, appeared in the market place as a minstrel and read and chanted, for he wanted the people to listen to his message.

The law was communicated to the people by having one person read it to an assembled group. Ezra read the laws to the people:

---

[1]Frederick G. Grant, *How to Read the Bible,* New York, Collier Books, by Morehouse-Gorham Company, 1956, p. 7.

See also Chloe Armstrong and Paul Brandes, *The Oral Interpretation of Literature,* New York, McGraw-Hill Book Company, Inc., 1963, Appendix B.

And all the people gathered as one man into the square before the Water Gate; and they told Ezra the scribe to bring the book of the law of Moses which the Lord had given to Israel. And Ezra the priest brought the law before the assembly, both men and women and all who could hear with understanding on the first day of the seventh month. And he read from it facing the square before the Water Gate from early morning until midday, in the presence of the men and the women and those who could understand; and the ears of all the people were attentive to the book of the law. And Ezra the scribe stood on a wooden pulpit which they had made for the purpose; and beside him stood Mattithiah, Shema, Anniah, Uriah, Hilkiah, and Maaseiah on his right hand; and Pedaiah, Mishael, Malchijah, Hashum, Hashbaddanah, Zechariah, and Meshullam on his left hand. And Ezra opened the book in the sight of all the people, for he was above all the people; and when he opened it, all the people stood. And Ezra blessed the Lord, the great God; and all the people answered, "Amen, Amen," lifting up their hands; and they bowed their heads and worshiped the Lord with their faces to the ground. Also Jeshua, Bani, Sherebiah, Jamin, Akkub, Shabbethai, Hodiah, Maaseiah, Kelita, Azariah, Jozabad, Hannan, Pelaiah, the Levites, helped the people to understand the law while the people remained in their places. And they read from the book, from the law of God, clearly, and they gave the sense, so that the people understood the reading.

(Nehemiah 8:1—8)

The historical books were read aloud and Herodotus recited or read his histories at Athens. The latter prophets read aloud their warnings and pronouncements. These writings were designed to be read or were given first orally and then written down.

The Psalms are songs composed to be read in unison, chanted, or sung. Often the Psalms were sung publicly. David himself was referred to as a minstrel and poet. Long before poems were committed to writing, they had been sung, recited, and handed down from generation to generation. In the time of the great kingdom of David and Solomon, the first period of the flowering of Hebrew literature, the Judean authors — whom scholars call the Yahwist — gathered the various stories and narratives together for a great work which related stories of the Hebrew people from their origin to the conflict of Canaan.

Psalms that were used in the temple services were sung by temple choirs, often accompanied by instrumental music. Responses were probably read by another group, or sometimes by the people.

Special festival hymns were sung at the yearly feasts. Psalm 81 was the New Year's Hymn. The congregation is gathered in the temple and the choir begins:

> *Sing aloud to God our strength;*
> > *shout for joy to the God of Jacob!*
> *Raise a song, sound the timbrel,*
> > *the sweet lyre with the harp.*
> *Blow the trumpet at the new moon,*
> > *at the full moon, on our feast day.*
> *For it is a statute for Israel,*
> > *an ordinance of the God of Jacob.*
> *He made it a decree in Joseph,*
> > *when he went out over the land of Egypt.*
> > > > *(Psalm 81:1—5)*

Prayers of thanksgiving for the harvest were offered. Psalm 67 was one of these:

> *May God be gracious to us and bless us*
> > *and make his face to shine upon us,*
> *that thy way may be known upon earth,*
> > *thy saving power among all nations.*
> *Let the peoples praise thee, O God;*
> > *let all the peoples praise thee!*
> *Let the nations be glad and sing for joy.*
> > *for thou dost judge the peoples with equity*
> > *and guide the nations upon earth.*
> *Let the peoples praise thee, O God;*
> > *let all the peoples praise thee!*
> *The earth has yielded its increase;*
> > *God, our God, has blessed us.*
> *God has blessed us;*
> > *let all the ends of the earth fear him!*
> > > > *(Psalm 67)*

The practice of reading the scriptures aloud even before they were scriptures in the canonical sense of the term possibly helped to determine their literary form when they were written. The priests recited the stories connected with their particular sanctuary. The shepherds told their tales of pastoral life; the peasants talked of agriculture and the city dwellers of urban life. Oral reading was part of their way of life. It was the means by which the culture and religious life could be crystallized and communicated from one group to another.

The letters of the New Testament were written to be read aloud at the meeting of the church, and were, therefore, public documents which needed to be written with great care. Many of the letters contained passages of lofty eloquence, which could not be fully appreciated until they were read aloud by a speaker. For example, although Paul wrote to one particular church, he knew that the letters would be circulated. At the end of Colossians he himself directed that neighboring churches should exchange the letters he had sent to them.

> *And when this letter has been read among you, have it read also in the church of the Laodiceans; and see that you read also the letter from Laodicea.*
>
> *(Colossians 4:1)*

The apostle knew that what he wrote would be copied and read by a large public; it is reasonable to assume he would put his best care into the writing, and use the language and structural form most adaptable for oral presentation.

One of the best known of the epistles is the thirteenth chapter of First Corinthians in which Paul makes a strong plea to his followers to come together in an atmosphere of love.

> *Though I speak with the tongues of men and of angels and have not charity, I am become as sounding brass or a tinkling cymbal.*

He closes his letter with these words:

> *And now abideth faith, hope, charity, these three: but the greatest of these is charity.*

Since Paul knew that much of the effectiveness of his message would depend on the success of its oral style, is it not reasonable to suppose that he wrote it for oral presentation?

The Revelation of St. John the Divine, the last book of the New Testament was specifically designed for reading aloud. As Dr. Grant points out, Revelation 22:18 is addressed to the "hearers":[2]

I warn every one who hears the words of the prophecy of this book: if any one adds to them, God will add to him the plagues described in this book.

There was a period before anything was written when all Christian teaching was by word of mouth. Thus the written Gospels were the result of this oral tradition.

The large majority of Christians only listened to poems in worship or learned their contents in instructions of church. Both letters and gospels were written for the most part with this end in view.

Thus, it is clear that reading aloud in synagogues and churches was certainly the ancient Jewish and early Christian practice. Moreover, today, the majority of the Jews and Christians hear the Bible read more often than they read it for themselves. Therefore, the translator of the Bible should have a feeling for oral reading and for appropriate liturgical style which makes use of rhythmic prose.

At present, when so much emphasis is put on speed in reading, we forget that the ancients read their philosophy aloud, taking time even in their private study to form each word, to pronounce it, and to hear how it sounded.

The Current Interest in Oral Reading

Just as the ancient Jewish and early Christian leaders read the Bible orally in their synagogues and churches, so today the oral reading of scripture is still an important part of our church services. It would be difficult to estimate how many of us hear the Bible read aloud more than we read it silently. For the past several years there has been an increasing interest in a study of the oral interpretation of biblical literature, manifested in the establishment of special courses in colleges and universities and in adult seminars for laymen and clergy held in conjunction with church conferences. Such an interest

[2]Grant, *op. cit.*, p. 21-22.

has arisen from two conclusions: first, that the quality of oral reading from scripture is in need of improvement, and second, that an investigation needs to be undertaken as to why the quality is substandard.

There are two factors which contribute to these conclusions: the reader's attitude toward the preparation of the material and his failure to recognize the scriptures as literature.

NEED FOR SPECIFIC PREPARATION

There are those who believe too much preparation will destroy the reading. They contend it will lack the freshness of interest, and the reading will become dull and monotonous. Others believe that reading from the printed page does not require thorough preparation; it is only when one memorizes the selection that preparation is necessary. Some readers contend that the material is there, and therefore their preparation is complete. Other oral readers fear "too much preparation and practice" will cause the presentation to be too dramatic or affective. Therefore, because of these attitudes, often no specific preparation in skill of readers is given for the oral presentation of the Bible.

The following is a scene fairly familiar to all of us. A group has assembed for a Sunday school class, a chapel program at school, or a meeting of a social or civic organization. The chairman decides that a short devotional is appropriate and calls on one of the members to read from the Bible. Without advance notice or preparation and with little or no hesitation, the chosen delegate turns to a chapter and reads – or at least stumbles along. Would the same person have attempted to read from one of the classics without any advanced preparation?[3] It is imperative that the Bible be read not only after a thorough study of the text, but also after a study of the available sources for preparation. To attempt reading without such background information is unfair to the listener, to the reader, and most of all to the book being interpreted – the Bible.

However, thorough preparation does not in itself guarantee effective presentation. In some instances the oral interpreter, in his eagerness to get the *message* of the scripture across, gets between the material and his audience. He may have made appropriate preparation, but the theme of his material is so close to him and he feels so

[3]Armstrong and Brandes, *op. cit.,* Appendix C.

strongly about it that he seems to be forcing an idea rather than sharing it. The interpreter should remember that, particularly in reading the Bible, the *message* will speak for itself if given the opportunity. It needs only an interpreter who will explore all the avenues to understanding and who will then step outside the material to communicate it to his audience.

BIBLE IS LITERATURE

A second reason for concluding that the quality of oral reading of scripture is sufficiently substandard to deserve searching study is that readers of the Bible fail to recognize the Scriptures as literature.

Frederic Kenyon says, "Apart from its religious value, the Bible is a collection of one of the great literatures of the world, one which has had vital influence on the development of our own literature."[4]

Throughout history great events experienced by a people have stimulated the creation of literature. This was true of the Hebrew people who, as Julius Bewer relates, "went through the fire of trial in the struggle with the foreign oppressor and came out of it a nation healed by a great king who governed the land he had wrested from the Canaanites."[5] They had a pride in their heroes who came through struggles, and they wanted to record happenings of the past — such was the beginning of their literature.

Many scholars have discussed the literary qualities of the Bible. James Moffatt refers to the literary art of Luke.[6] Ernest Findley Scott discussed the literary style of the different writers of the New Testament. He described Paul as a man of literary culture; he compared his way of presenting his ideas to the method Shakespeare used in his later plays. He stated that Paul ranks among the world's great writers. He described Luke as a literary artist.[7]

Buckner Trawick states that we may regard the Bible as an anthology of ancient Hebrew and early Christian religious literature,

---

[4]Sir Frederic Kenyon, *The Reading of the Bible,* London, John Murray, 1944-45, p. 92.

[5]Julius A. Bewer, *The Literature of The Old Testament,* 3rd Edition revised by Emil G. Kraeling, New York and London, Columbia University Press, 1962, p. 23.

[6]James Moffatt, *Introduction to the Literature of the New Testament,* The International Theological Library, New York, Charles Scribner's Sons, 1911, p. 8.

[7]Ernest Findley Scott, *The Literature of the New Testament,* New York, Columbia University Press, 1932, p. 6.

as two or three books (Old Testament, Apocrypha, and New Testament), or as a unified, single work of literature.[8]

The Bible presents not only collections of the greatest of literature, but also all the different types of literature, for as Dr. Grant has stated, "God does not spurn or disregard human thought and imagination, poetry, folklore, history, wisdom, law, prophecy, or philosophy; instead he uses it, improves it, fulfills it, and thus speaks to mankind not only in their own tongues but through their own voices — the familiar voices of their holiest and best, their saints, apostles, martyrs."[9]

Bewer states that "poetry and religion go together. In moments of religious experience, whether the soul is at one with God or seeking Him, its utterances often take poetic form; common prose is not adequate to express its joy or its longing; in rhythmic rise and cadence praise and prayer flow forth, revealing man's deepest feelings and desires. That is why the Psalms are so important, for we have here a singularly profound revelation of the inner life of God's people."[10]

If the Bible is literature, it is governed by the principles of literature. Dr. S. S. Curry emphasizes this point in his work *Vocal and Literary Interpretation of the Bible.* "There is a strange feeling that to regard the Bible as literature is in some way to degrade it. On the contrary, the more exalted a book the higher and more sublime it is, the more does it belong to literature." Dr. Curry continues by asking questions — Does a lyric dease to be a lyric because it is in the Bible? Does a dramatic passage lose its character because it is sacred?"[11] According to Aristotle the difference between history and poetry implies a higher truth and higher seriousness. If we can accept this explanation, portions of the Bible must be not only literature but great literature, the most lyrical poetry.

Oral interpretation of the Bible implies as part of the preparation a thorough study of it as literature. An interpreter must understand the Book of Ruth for its qualities as a short story if he is to

---

[8]Buckner B. Trawick, *The Bible As Literature,* New York, Barnes and Noble, Inc., 1963, p. 15.

[9]Grant, *op. cit.,* p. 65.

[10]Bewer, *op. cit.,* p. 359.

[11]S. S. Curry, *Voice and Literary Interpretation of the Bible,* Hodder and Stoughton, New York, George H. Doran Co., 1905, p. 47.

understand its historical and biblical meaning. The same narrative elements are used in the Books of Esther and Job that are found in other narratives. Thus to approach the Bible as literature will give insight into its spiritual values.

With the rise of literary prophets such as Amos and Hosea, a new era in literature and religion was born. These prophets not only produced a new class of literature, but ushered in the greatest movement in the spiritual history of mankind.

The excellence of literary style and the use of clear rhythmic lines are characteristic of these literary prophets. Thus Bewer describes the ability of Nahum to create word pictures as superb.[12]

Sir Frederic Kenyon, in urging his readers to read the Bible said, "Read it with interest as history, with admiration as literature, and with the profoundest reverence as the record of the progressive training of mankind in its knowledge of God up to the dispensation of the mystery which from all ages hath been hid in God who created all things."[13]

In reading and studying the Bible, you will soon realize that much of it is poetry. The Old Testament is full of lyric passages. The historical books are full of poems; so is the Torah, especially Genesis; the prophetic books are primarily in poetic form, as the Revised Version, the Revised Standard Version, and the King James Version reveals. Job, the Psalms, Proverbs, and even much of Ecclesiastes are poetry. In the New Testament many of Christ's sayings contain poetic elements. The long discourses in John are all poetic; many of the quotations of Paul and Hebrews are from Poems, and the hymns in the book of Revelation are examples of early Christian poetry.

The reading of poetry makes special demands upon the communicator both in the study and presentation. Aristotle said that poetry is different; it is "more philosophical and more serious than history," and requires imagination and insight for its understanding and for the discovery and disclosure of its "message." Poetry deals with general truths, rather than with particular facts. "Poetry," according to Laurence Perrine, "is a kind of language that says more and says it more intensely than does ordinary language."[14] Further discussion of poetry will be given later, but the point to be established here is

[12]Bewer, *op. cit.*, p. 148.

[13]Kenyon, *op. cit.*, p. 92.

[14]Laurence Perrine, *Sound and Sense An Introduction to Poetry,* New York, Harcourt Brace and Company, Inc., 1956, p. 3.

that much of the Bible is poetry and, therefore, is especially suited for oral reading.

The Hebrew literature is one of the most rhythmical of all literatures. Moses and his people sang their triumphant song. The opening words are perhaps the oldest piece of literature in the Bible.

Then Moses and the people of Israel sang this song to the Lord, saying,

I will sing to the Lord, for he has triumphed gloriously;
    the horse and his rider he has thrown into the sea.
The Lord is my strength and my song,
    and he has become my salvation;
    this is my God, and I will praise him,
    my father's God, and I will exalt him.
The Lord is a man of war;
    the Lord is his name.
Pharaoh's chariots and his host he cast into the sea;
    and his picked officers are sunk in the Red Sea.
The floods cover them;
    they went down into the depths like a stone.
Thy right hand, O Lord, glorious in power,
    thy right hand, O Lord, shatters the enemy.
In the greatness of thy majesty thou overthrowest thy adversaries;
    thou sendest forth thy fury, it consumes them like stubble.
At the blast of thy nostrils the waters piled up,
    the floods stood up in a heap;
    the deeps congealed in the heart of the sea.
The enemy said, 'I will pursue, I will overtake,
    I will divide the spoil, my desire shall have its fill of them.
    I will draw my sword, my hand shall destroy them.'
Thou didst blow with thy wind, the sea covered them;
    they sank as lead in the mighty waters.
Who is like thee, O Lord, among the gods?
    Who is like thee, majestic in holiness,
    terrible in glorious deeds, doing wonders?
Thou didst stretch out thy right hand, the earth swallowed them.
Thou has led in thy steadfast love the people whom thou hast redeemed,
    thou hast guided them by thy strength to thy holy abode.
The peoples have heard, they tremble;

pangs have seized on the inhabitants of Philistia.
Now are the chiefs of Edom dismayed;
the leaders of Moab, trembling seizes them;
all the inhabitants of Canaan have melted away.
Terror and dread fall upon them;
because of the greatness of thy arm, they are as still as a stone,
'til thy people, O Lord, pass by,
till the people pass by whom thou has purchased.
Thou wilt bring them in, and plant them on thy own mountain,
the place, O Lord, which thou has made for thy abode,
the sanctuary, O Lord, which thy hands have established.
The Lord will reign for ever and ever.
(Exodus 15:1—18)

The book of Psalms is religious poetry of the best quality. The Twenty-third Psalm "says more and says it more intensely than ordinary language."[15]

The Lord is my shepherd, I shall not want;
He makes me lie down in green pastures: he leads me beside still
waters.
He restores my soul; he leads me in paths of righteousness for his
name's sake.
Even though I walk through the valley of the shadow of death, I
fear no evil: for thou art with me; thy rod and thy staff, they
comfort me.
Thou preparest a table before me in the presence of my enemies.
Thou annointest my head with oil, my cup overflows.
Surely goodness and mercy shall follow me all the days of my
life;
and I shall dwell in the house of the Lord for ever.

The recording of the deaths of Jonathan and Saul is one of the finest poems in the Bible. It is a dirge laden with deep personal sorrow.

The beauty of Israel is slain upon thy high places.
How are the mighty fallen!....
Saul and Jonathan were lovely and pleasant in their lives,

[15]*Ibid.*

And in their death they were not divided.
They were swifter than eagles,
They were stronger than lions. . . .
How are the mighty fallen in the midst of the battle!
O Jonathan, thou wast slain in thine high places.
I am distressed for thee, my brother Jonathan:
Very pleasant has thou been unto me:
Thy love to me was wonderful,
Passing the love of woman.
                                        (II Samuel 1:19–26)

Song of Solomon frequently referred to as Song of Songs is a group of love songs of much beauty. They are usually short and associated with joy in the beauties of nature. "We may thus regard the Song of Songs as a collection of small lyrics which have been strung together without any special plan. Some may be old and of Israelite origin as references to northern areas and places suggest."[16]

One great contribution of the Song of Songs is that it brings to life for us the otherwise rather submerged female psyche of Hebrew antiquity. Laws and customs left little room for the marriage of inclination. It is an isolated instance if we hear of Michal's love for David (I Samuel 18:20). But in the Song of Songs we get the picture of the maiden who idealizes a lover to whom she belongs, body and soul.

My beloved is mine and I am his,
*   he pastures his flock among the lilies.*
Until the day breathes and the shadows flee,
*   Turn, my beloved, be like a gazelle*
*   or a young stag on rugged mountains.*
                                        (Song of Songs 2:16–17)

The pain of love, too, comes to the surface in the repeated warning:

I adjure you, O daughters of Jerusalem
*   by the gazelles or the hinds of the field*
that you stir not up or awaken love
*   until it please...*
                                        (Song of Songs 2:7)

[16]Bewer, *op. cit.,* p. 355.

The universally human background, in combination with the exotic Oriental imagery that is poured forth here, gives the Song an appeal that leads many to consider it the greatest love poetry in all literature.

Isaiah was a great poet, and he wrote only in poetry. With the use of figurative language he wrote passages of exquisite beauty as shown in the following selections:

Who has measured the waters in the hollow of his hand
and marked off the heavens with a span,
enclosed the dust of the earth in a measure
and weighed the mountains in scales
and the hills in a balance?
Who has directed the Spirit of the Lord,
or as his counselor has instructed him?
Whom did he consult for his enlightenment,
and who taught him the path of justice,
and taught him knowledge,
and showed him the way of understanding?
(Isaiah 40:12—14)

Sing to the Lord a new song,
his praise from the end of the earth!
Let the sea roar and all that fills it,
the coastlands and their inhabitants.
Let the desert and its cities lift up their voice,
the villages that Kedar inhabits;
let the inhabitants of Sela sing for joy, let them
shout from the top of the mountains.
Let them give glory to the Lord,
and declare his praise in the coastlands.
(Isaiah 42:10—12)

"Listen to me, my people,
and give ear to me, my nation;
for a law will go forth from me, and my justice
for a light to the peoples.
My deliverance draws near speedily,
my salvation has gone forth,
and my arms will rule the peoples;

the coastlands wait for me,
  and for my arm they hope.
Lift up your eyes to the heavens,
  and look at the earth beneath;
for the heavens will vanish like smoke,
    the earth will wear out like a garment,
    and they who dwell in it will die like gnats;
but my salvation will be for ever,
    and my deliverance will never be ended.
                          (Isaiah 51:4—6)

The poetry of Jeremiah belongs to the finest in the literature of the world. In a mood of great grief for Jerusalem, the prophet composed a group of poems addressed directly to the people. "The most moving of all," according to Bewer is "his oracle to the women." [17]

Hear the word of Yahweh, O ye women,
  and let your ear receive the word of His mouth;
And teach your daughters wailing,
  every one her neighbor lamentation:
"Death is come up into our windows,
  it is entered into our palaces,
To cut off the children from without,
  the young men from the streets.
"The dead bodies of men shall fall
  upon the open field,
As the sheaves after the harvestman;
  and none shall gather them.
                          (Jeremiah 9:20—22)

My anguish, my anguish! I writhe in pain!
  Oh, the walls of my heart!
My heart is beating wildly;
  I cannot keep silent;
for I hear the sound of the trumpet,
  the alarm of war.
Destruction upon destruction is reported,
  for the whole land is laid waste:

[17]Bewer, *op. cit.,* p. 160-161.

Suddenly are my tents destroyed,
   and my curtains in a moment.
How long shall I see the standard,
   and hear the sound of the trumpet?
                              (Jeremiah 4:19–21)

The whole second part of the book of Hosea is poetry. His imagination is vivid, his style is allegorically picturesque.

For they sow the wind,
   and they shall reap the whirlwind.
The standing grain has no heads,
   it shall yield no meal;
if it were to yield,
   aliens would devour it.
Israel is swallowed up;
   already they are among the nations as a
   useless vessel.
                              (Hosea 9:7–8)

When Israel was a child, I loved him,
   and out of Egypt I called my son.
The more I called them,
   the more they went from me;
they kept sacrificing to the Baals,
   and burning incense to idols.
Yet it was I who taught Ephraim to walk,
   I took them up in my arms;
   but they did not know that I healed them.
I led them with cords of compassion,
   with bands of love,
   and I became to them as one who eases the
   yoke on their jaws,
   and I bent down to them and fed them.
They shall return to the land of Egypt,
   and Assyria shall be their king,
   because they have refused to return to me.
                              (Hosea 11:1–5)

Nahum uses word pictures to create his poetic effects. Note the poetic element of imagery:

Woe to the bloody city,
   all full of lies and booty —
   no end to the plunder!
The crack of whip, and rumble of whee,
   galloping horse and bounding chariot!
Horsemen charging,
   flashing sword and glittering spear,
hosts of slain,
   heaps of corpses,
dead bodies without end —
   they stumble over the bodies!
And all for the the countless harlotries of the harlot,
   graceful and of deadly charms,
who betrays nations with her harlotries,
   and peoples with her charms.
Behold, I am against you,
   says the Lord of hosts,
   and will lift up your skirts over your face;
and I will let nations look on your nakedness
   and kingdoms on your shame.
                                   (Nahum 3:1—5)

Part of Ecclesiastes can be classified as poetry for it contains many poetic elements: the choice of words, the phrased form, and the rhythm. All of these factors are soon discovered by the reader, and the sound within the word adds much to the mood and attitude of the selection.

There is an evil which I have seen under the sun, and it lies heavy upon men: a man to whom God gives wealth, possessions, and honor so that he lacks nothing of all that he desires; yet God does not give power to enjoy them, but a stranger enjoys them; this is vanity; it is a sore affliction. If a man begets a hundred children, and lives many years, so that the days of his years are many, but he does not enjoy life's good things, and also has no burial, I say that an untimely birth is better off than he. For it comes into vanity and goes into darkness, and in darkness its name is covered; moreover, it has not seen the sun or known anything; yet it finds rest rather than he.
                                   (Ecclesiastes 6:1—5)

A good name is better than precious ointment;
    and the day of death, than the day of birth.
It is better to go to the house of mourning
    than to go to the house of feasting;
for this is the end of all men,
    and the living will lay it to heart.
Sorrow is better than laughter,
    for by sadness of countenance the heart is made glad.
The heart of the wise is in the house of mourning;
    but the heart of fools is in the house of mirth.
                                       (Ecclesiastes 7:1–4)

The high development of the art of poetic expression found in the early poems of the Old Testament indicates that a long training must have preceded the earliest literature. Poetry was the earliest form of literary expression in Hebrew; therefore, it is only natural that we find so much of the Bible written in poetic form. But poetry is not confined to the Old Testament, there are many poetic passages in the New Testament. Many of Christ's statements as recorded by Luke are poetry.

Now as they went on their way, he entered a village; and a woman named Martha received him into her house.
                                       (Luke 10:38)

And he said to them, "When you pray, say:
    Father, hallowed be thy name. Thy kingdom come. Give us each day our daily bread; and forgive us our sins, for we ourselves forgive every one who is indebted to us; and lead us not into temptation."
                                       (Luke 11:2–4)

And that servant who knew his master's will, but did not make ready or act according to his will, shall receive a severe beating. But he who did not know, and did what deserved a beating, shall receive a light beating. Every one to whom much is given, of him will much be required; and of him demand the more.
I came to cast fire upon the earth; and would that it were already kindled! I have a baptism to be baptized with; and how I am constrained until it is accomplished!
                                       (Luke 12:47–50)

The discourses found in Acts are poetic.

For David says concerning him,
   "I saw the Lord always before me,
   for he is at my right hand that I may not be shaken;
   therefore my heart was glad, and my tongue rejoiced;
   moreover my flesh will dwell in hope.
   For thou wilt not abandon my soul to Hades,
   nor let thy Holy One see corruption.
   Thou hast made known to me the ways of life;
   thou wilt make me full of gladness with thy presence."
                        (Acts 2:25—28)

   Heaven is my throne,
   and earth my footstool.
   What house will you build for me,
      says the Lord,
   or what is the place of my rest?
   Did not my hand make all these things?
                        (Acts 7:49—50)

Paul's letters, although they often contained persuasive elements or instructive information, are poetic in style and language.

Though I speak with the tongues of men and of angels, and have not charity, I am become as sounding brass, or a tinkling cymbal. And though I have the gift of prophecy, and understand all mysteries, and all knowledge; and
though I have all faith, so that I could remove mountains, and have not charity, I am nothing.
And though I bestow all my goods to feed the poor,
and though I give my body to be burned, and have not charity, it profiteth me nothing.   KJV
                        (I Corinthians 13:1—3)

Some of the best of early Christian poetry is found in Hebrews and the book of Revelation.

For he finds fault with them when he says:
   "The days will come, says the Lord,
   when I will establish a new covenant

with the house of Israel and
with the house of Judah;
not like the covenant that I made with their
fathers on the day when I took them by the
hand to lead them out of the land of Egypt;
for they did not continue in my covenant,
and so I paid no heed to them, says the Lord.
This is the convenant that I will make
with the house of Israel
after those days, says the Lord:
I will put my laws into their minds,
and write them on their hearts,
and I will be their God,
and they shall be my people.
And they shall not teach every one his fellow
or every one his brother, saying,
"Know the Lord," for all shall know me,
from the least of them to the greatest.
For I will be merciful toward their iniquities,
and I will remember their sins no more."
(Hebrews 8:8—12)

And I saw the beast and the kings of the earth with their armies
gathered to make war against him who sits upon the horse and
against his army. And the beast was captured, and with it the
false prophet who in its presence had worked the signs by which
he deceived those who had received the mark of the beast and
those who worshiped its image. These two were thrown alive into
the lake of fire that burns with brimstone.
(Revelation 19:19—20)

I am the Alpha and the Omega, the first and the last, the
beginning and the end.
Blessed are those who wash their robes, that they may have the
right to the tree of life and that they may enter the city by the
gates. Outside are the dogs and sorcerers and fornicators and
murderers and idolaters, and every one who loves and practices
falsehood.
"I Jesus have sent my angel to you with this testimony for the

churches. I am the root and the offspring of David, the bright morning star."
The spirit and the Bride say, "Come." And let him who hears say, "Come." And let him who is thirsty come, let him who desires take the water of life without price.
I warn every one who hears the words of the prophecy of this book.

(Revelation 22:13–18)

Throughout the Bible, both Old Testament and New, one finds poetic literature. Different types of lyric, narrative, and dramatic poetry make up a large portion of the biblical literature.

Poetry by its nature is to be read orally. The poet's ear is sensitive to the sound of words. Poetry is written to be heard, its meaning is conveyed through sound, as well as through context. The sounding of words helps both the reader and the audience to feel the mood of the poem. Rhythm and sound cooperate to produce what we call the music of poetry. Poetry therefore should be read aloud. As Lee states: "Poetry reaches its ultimate when it is read aloud."[18]

THE CONTRIBUTION OF ORAL READING TO LITERATURE

Most of the teachers and writers of oral interpretation for the past several years have pointed out the contribution that oral reading can make for understanding and appreciation of literature.

The ability to read aloud in an effective manner can clarify and emphasize the meaning of literature. Oral reading provides a stimulus for appreciation of material. The reader has the feeling of sharing his understanding and insight with the audience.

The ancient and medieval scholars recognized the importance of reading aloud. Socrates taught by conversation. Plato wrote down his thoughts in dialogue form so that the interpersonal relationship could be retained. Aristotle kept the tradition by treating knowledge as basically oral.

The reading aloud can add much to the understanding and appreciation of biblical literature. Dr. Grant in urging the study of the literature of the Bible points out that "there have been inter-

---

[18]Charlotte I. Lee, *Oral Interpretation,* Second Edition, Boston, Houghton Mifflin Company, 1959, p. 387.

preters of Biblical poetry who lacked appreciation for any kind of poetry whatsoever. There have been expounders of its great literature who really cared nothing for literature in general."[19] Oral reading of the Bible can aid in developing this appreciation. It permits such elements as tempo, volume, and diction to restore the aural component to literature. This can intensify the mood and thought of the material. Reading aloud through effective use of voice can vitalize the experience of literature. Appreciation of any literature often comes from response to the emotion. Oral reading can intensify this emotion in literature and deepen the appreciation. When the Bible is being read by a good reader, it may become more vividly realized by a member of the audience simply because he is listening to it with other people. Often one may listen to a familiar scripture with only slight contemplation of the meaning; but an effective reader, by sharing his understanding of the material, can give new meaning to the audience and discover new meaning for himself. As Geiger says, "Good presentation helps an audience to understand the text, but the performer's work helps him to understand the text also."[20] This process can become a cycle, the reader can use oral interpretation as a means for his understanding of his material, and in turn he can share his additional appreciation with his listener. "Emotion in poetry is to be shared, not explained, appreciation and understanding come from sharing."[21]

A good oral interpreter can do much to create proper mood and atmosphere for reverence and worship by reading aloud the Bible. His presentation focuses attention on the scripture and thereby emphasizes the oral reading as a vital part of the worship.

Summary

We have been concerned in this chapter with showing the student of the Bible the value of the oral reading approach. In presenting the values and contribution of oral reading, it is not the intention of the writer to claim that this method is the answer to the understanding

[19]Grant, *op. cit.*, p. 15.

[20]Don Geiger, *The Sound, Sense and Performance of Literature,* Chicago, Scott Foresman and Company, 1963, p. 2.

[21]Perrine, *op. cit.*, p. 19.

of the Bible. Oral interpretation of the scriptures will not make Biblical scholars of readers of the Bible.

Moreover, the value and role of silent reading are in no way to be disparaged. There are occasions when the individual will want to read the Bible silently, reflectively, and meditatively. But there are unique values gained by the person who seriously studies how to read the Bible aloud, and then develops his skills to read effectively. Much of the value of oral reading of the Bible belongs to the listener, for it is he who shares with the knowledge and skill of the reader.

Chapter Two

PREPARATION FOR UNDERSTANDING

The books of the Bible, like all selections of literature, must be read in the light of their own times, and with an understanding of the purposes of the writings. Samuel Taylor Coleridge once said, "Read the Bible as you would any other book, and you will discover how unlike it is to other."[1]

Biographical and Historical Background

It would be helpful for the reader to review briefly the historical background for the setting of the Bible.

The Hebrew Nation (Palestine) in Biblical times was encircled by and subjected to great empires such as the Egyptian, Assyrian, Babylonian, and Persian. It became a part of each and absorbed culture from each, and yet kept many of its own customs and traditions. Egypt developed an advanced civilization which had cultural influences on the Hebrews. When Alexander the Great conquered Persia about 331 B.C., the Greek civilization was forced upon the Hebrews of Palestine. Thus Hellenic culture was a strong influence on the Hebrews. The influence of Greek philosophy and drama was reflected in thoughts of Jesus and early Christians.

It is evident that the location and climate of Palestine had a great influence on the intellectual and material life of its inhabitants. Much of the soil was hilly and poor. From the middle of the 18th century B.C. to the beginning of the Christian era, the country was overrun by one power after another. This fact explains to the reader the prayers of the people, asking for deliverance from the indignities and persecutions to which they were subjected. The Old Testament reflects the courage of the people and their faith that God would

[1]Grant, *op. cit.*, p. 65.

deliver them. The oral reader will reflect this mood and feeling when reading from parts of the Old Testament.

According to Genesis, the land of Palestine was given to Abraham and his descendants by divine convenant. The Hebrews probably did not become a nation until the Exodus from Egypt. After a generation of wandering in the Wilderness, they finally reached Palestine.

The first Israelites were a semi-nomadic tribe who lived chiefly in tents, who raised herds of sheep and goats, and who moved about as the need for pastureland or the pressure of hostile neighbors dictated. With the passage of time and their entrance into the Promised Land of Canaan (which they conquered about 1200 B.C.) the Hebrews became more sedentary, continuing their pastoral economy but devoting more attention to agriculture and trade, both of which developed and flourished.

The earliest society was patriarchal and the father had almost absolute powers over his wife and children. Conditions of life were hard; when the perils were overcome so that the nation survived, the people attributed their survival to divine intervention. As in all literature, much of the historical and cultural background of the people is reflected in Biblical literature.

Translations of the Bible

In studying the Bible it would be an advantage to know the Greek and Hebrew languages, but this knowledge is out of reach for the majority of readers. Although no translation can reproduce the exact *sound* or *word* of the original, it is reasonable to believe that the English translations reflect the original style of the Bible. But the study and comparison of the different translations can be very beneficial; it can give greater insight into the meaning of the selection read. This approach is available to all. For example, compare the three different translations of the Thirteenth Chapter of I Corinthians.

KING JAMES VERSION
Though I speak with the tongues of men and of angels, and have not charity, I am become as sounding brass, or a tinkling cymbal.

And though I have the gift of prophecy, and understand all mysteries, and all knowledge; and though I have all faith, so that I could remove mountains, and have not charity, I am nothing.
And though I bestow all my goods to feed the poor.
and though I give my body to be burned, and have not charity, it profiteth me nothing.
Charity suffereth long, and is kind; charity envieth not; charity vaunteth not itself, is not puffed up,
Doth not behave itself unseemly, seeketh not her own, is not easily provoked, thinketh no evil;
Rejoiceth not in iniquity, but rejoiceth in the truth;
Beareth all things, believeth all things, hopeth all things, endureth all things.
Charity never faileth: but whether there be prophecies, they shall fail; where there be tongues, they shall cease; whether there be knowledge, it shall vanish away.
For we know in part, and we prophesy in part. But when that which is perfect is come, then that which is in part shall be done away.
When I was a child, I spake as a child, I understood as a child, I thought as a child: but when I became a man, I put away childish things.
For now we see through a glass, darkly; but then face to face; now I know in part; but then shall I know even as also I am known.
And now abideth faith, hope, charity, these three; but the greatest of these is charity.

TRANSLATION BY JAMES MOFFATT

I speak with the tongues of men and of angels, but if I have no love, I am a noisy gong or a clanging cymbal;
I may prophesy, fathom all mysteries and secret lore,
I may have such absolute faith that I can move hills from their place, but if I have no love, I count for nothing;
I may distribute all I possess in charity,
I may give up my body to be burnt, but if I have no love, I make nothing of it.
Love is very patient, very kind. Love knows no jealousy; love makes no parade, gives itself no airs, is never rude, never selfish,

never irritated, <u>never resentful</u>; love is never glad when others go wrong, love is gladdened by goodness, always slow to expose, always eager to believe the best, always hopeful, always patient. Love never disappears.

As for prophesying, it will be superseded; as for 'tongues,' they will cease; as for knowledge, it will be superseded. For we only know bit by bit, and we only prophesy bit by bit; but when the perfect comes, the imperfect will be superseded.

When I was a child, I talked like a child, I thought like a child, I argued like a child; now that I am a man, I am done with childish ways.

At present we only see the baffling reflections in a mirror, but then it will be face to face; at present I am learning bit by bit, but then I shall understand, as all along I have myself been understood.

Thus 'faith and hope and love last on, these three' but the greatest of all is love.

REVISED STANDARD VERSION

If I speak in the tongues of men and of angels, but have not <u>love</u>, I am a <u>noisy gong</u> or a <u>clanging cymbal</u>. And if I have prophetic powers, and understand all mysteries and all knowledge, and if I have all faith, so as to remove mountains, but have not love, I am nothing. If I give away all I have, and if I deliver my body to be burned, but have not love, I gain nothing.

Love is patient and kind; love is not jealous or boastful; it is not arrogant or rude. Love does not insist on its own way; it is not irritable or resentful; it does not rejoice at wrong, but rejoices in the right. Love bears all things, believes all things, hopes all things, endures all things.

Love never ends; as for prophecies, they will pass away; as for tongues, they will cease; as for knowledge, it will pass away. For our knowledge is imperfect and our prophecy is imperfect; but when the perfect comes, the imperfect will pass away. When I was a child, I spoke like a child; when I became a man, I gave up childish ways. For now we see in a mirror dimly, but then face to face. Now I know in part; then I shall understand fully, even as I have been fully understood. So faith, hope, love abide, these three; but the greatest of these is love.

Note the choice of words used in each translation. How do the sounds of the underscored words contribute to the meaning of the verse? Compare the different images created by the three different translations.

Though I speak with the tongues of men and of angels, and have not <u>charity</u>, I am become as <u>sounding brass</u>, or a <u>tinkling</u> cymbal.

— — — — — — — — —

I speak with the tongues of men and of angels, but if I have no <u>love</u>, I am a <u>noisy gong</u> or a <u>clanging cymbal;</u>

— — — — — — — — .

If I speak in the tongues of men and of angels, but have not <u>love</u>, I am a <u>noisy gong</u> or a <u>clanging cymbal</u>.

Compare the explanation of charity-love as given by the three translations.

Chairty suffereth long, <u>and</u> is kind; charity envieth not; charity vaunteth not itself, is not puffed up,
Doth not behave itself unseemly, seeketh not her own, is not easily provoked, thinketh no evil;
Rejoiceth not in iniquity, but rejoiceth in the truth;
Beareth all things, believeth all things, hopeth all things, endureth all things.
Charity never faileth:

— — — — — — — — —

Love is very patient, very kind. Love knows no jealousy; love makes no parade, gives itself no airs, is never rude, never selfish, never irritated, <u>never resentful</u>; love is never glad when others go wrong, love is gladened by goodness, always slow to expose, always eager to believe the best, always hopeful, always patient. Love never disappears.

— — — — — — — —

Love is patient and kind; love is not jealous or boastful; it is not arrogant or rude. Love does not insist on its own way; it is not irritable or resentful; it does not rejoice at wrong, but rejoices in the right. Loves bears all things, believes all things, hopes all things, endures all things.
Love never ends;

The three different statements of the concept of love give more insight into the meaning. The student should read the three different translations several times, comparing the language and structure of each. Now, return to the translation of your choice and reread it. Did you gain a richer experience from the study?

The question is often asked, which translation is the best for study and oral reading. Who can say which is the best? There are no set rules. The version used must depend upon the occasion, the audience, and the reader. The oral reader may prefer one translation for a particular scripture, and choose a different translation for another. Although the appreciation of some people may be disturbed by a new or a different translation, most listeners will accept the choice of the sincere oral reader.

Trawick emphasizes this point. "There are several versions of the Bible now in use in the churches and homes of English-speaking people all over the world. Each has its own particular merits and shortcomings, all are worthy of the respect and attention of students of literature."[2]

Biblical Commentaries and Critics

There are many great scholars in the field of theology. Men throughout history have spent their lives studying and writing about the Bible. The present time is no exception. Outstanding professors and scholars are studying and sharing their knowledge and insight with all who will read their books. The oral reader in preparing to read from the Bible will do well to study the books of these scholars. Would any one reject the help of scholars in studying any other piece of great literature, ancient or modern? The expert who has spent ten, twenty, or fifty years studying a particular author or a certain literary work can give more of the understanding and meaning of the material than the casual reader of the same author or selection. This approach does not mean or even imply that for your own private religious benefit you cannot read the Bible and interpret it as best you can: one can and should. But there is no conflict between a casual reading and the scholarly search for its deepest and most profound meaning. Anyone can read Shakespeare, Milton, or a

[2]Trawick, *op. cit.*, p. 31.

modern poet, and enjoy each; but for aid in our study we turn to the critics and scholars for assistance. As the Bible itself says, "Come let us reason together." (Isaiah 1:18) And as Professor Grant states in referring to the approach of understanding the Bible, "It speaks clearest when we study it closest, and try to find what it meant when first written; to the authors themselves, and to those who heard it read to them for the first time — or the hundredth."[3]

The Bible Itself

In the study of the Bible the most important source is the Bible itself. Read the scriptures in a receptive mood. To understand each book or chapter you need to be familiar with its general purpose and the nature of its content and the setting in which it was written. In the analysis of biblical literature one should ask the following questions: Who is speaking? To whom is he speaking? What was said and in what mood? James Moffatt in his introduction to his translation of the Bible emphasizes the need for this type of study in his statement, "Who were these people? When and how did they live? What were the forms and function of their literature? Such are the questions which require to be answered before we can read the Bible intelligently."[4] Answers to these questions will help to clarify the meaning of scriptures and therefore will be the key to more effective reading.

BACKGROUND

In attempting to communicate the same message, or at least the same spirit and basic content of the message as it was written in the original, to his audience, the reader must understand the purpose and nature of the particular scripture. It is necessary to understand the entire book and the relationship of the selection to the book. The Bible cannot be studied as separate individual sections, but rather it must be considered as a unique whole with each part related to every other part.

---

[3]Grant, *op. cit.*, p. 66.
[4]James Moffatt, *The Bible A New Translation*, Harper and Brothers Publishers, New York and London, 1954, p. 7 of Introduction.

If you are preparing to read the Ten Commandments from
Exodus 20:1-17, you would need to know that Moses is speaking. He
is giving a code of laws by which the people will be governed. But for
a broader understanding you would need to know the relationship of
this particular part to the total development of the Hebrew history.
You should be able to answer the following questions: What events
had taken place before the laws were given? Why and how was Moses
chosen to give the laws? Were the laws ever modified or changed; and
if so, how and by whom and what influence did the laws have on the
total religious and historical life of the Hebrew people? The 20th
chapter of Exodus, or even the complete book itself, is not an
isolated portion of the Bible, but an intricate part related to the
happenings before the time the laws were given, and to the happenings after the laws were given and, therefore, must be studied in its
historical perspective.

And God spoke all these words saying,
  "I am the Lord your God, who brought you out of the land of
  Egypt, out of the house of Bondage.
  "You shall have no other gods before me.
  "You shall not make for yourself a graven image, or any
  likeness of anything that is in heaven above, or that is in the
  earth beneath, or that is in the water under the earth; You
  shall not bow down to them or serve them; for I the Lord
  your God am a jealous God, visiting the iniquity of the fathers
  upon the children to the third and the fourth generation of
  those who hate me, but showing steadfast love to thousands
  of those who love me and keep my commandments.
  "You shall not take the name of the Lord your God in vain;
  for the Lord will not hold him guiltless who takes his name in
  vain.
  "Remember the sabbath day, to keep it holy. Six days you
  shall labor, and do all your work; but the seventh day is a
  sabbath to the Lord your God; in it you shall not do any
  work, you, or your son, or your daughter, your manservant,
  or your maidservant, or your cattle, or the sojourner who is
  within your gates; for in six days the Lord made heaven and
  earth, the sea, and all that is in them, and rested the seventh
  day; therefore the Lord blessed the sabbath day and hallowed
  it.

"Honor your father and your mother, that your days may be long in the land which the Lord your God gives you.
"You shall not kill.
"You shall not commit adultery.
"You shall not steal.
"You shall not bear false witness against your neighbor.
"You shall not covet your neighbor's house; you shall not covet your neighbor's wife, or his manservant, or his maidservant, or his ox, or his ass, or anything that is your neighbor's."

It will be helpful for the student to remember these laws were for pastoral, agricultural people. The law set forth their duties to God and to other men. To know something of the character of Moses would also be helpful to the reader. Trawick describes him as a superb combination of humility and boldness. He is humble as is shown in his doubting his own ability; yet he is bold enough to upbraid God himself for giving him the burden of leading the (children of Israel).[5] The more you understand of the man speaking, the more you may understand what he is saying.

In preparing to read Exodus 20, you should be aware that the author is speaking, giving factual material in a direct forceful manner.

The book of Deuteronomy, although it also is dealing with the law and is more or less a restatement of Mosaic law, is very different in mood to the mood expressed in Exodus 20. The oral reader in presenting this part of the Bible to an audience must reflect on the cadence of this literature. The author makes use of vowel sounds in the special choice of words as he speaks to laymen.

The Lord our God said to us in Horeb, "Horeb, you have stayed long enough at this mountain, turn and take your journey, and go to the hill country of the Amorites, and to all their neighbors in the Arabah, in the hill country and in the lowland, and in the Negeb, and by the seacoast, the land of the Canaanites, and Lebanon, as far as the great river Euphrates. Behold, I have set the land before you; go in and take possession of the land which the Lord swore to your fathers, to Abraham, to Isaac, and to Jacob, to give to them and do their descendents after them."
(Deuteronomy 1:6—8)

[5] Trawick, *op. cit.,* p. 59.

The author continues to set forth the law to the people, at the same time giving explicit instructions as to how it is to be carried out. The reader will notice the change of mood as expressed in such phrases as:

These are the statutes and ordinances which you shall be careful to do in the land which the Lord, the God of your fathers, has given you to possess, all the days that you live upon the earth. You shall surely destroy all the places where the nations whom you shall dispossess served their gods, upon the high mountains and upon the hills and under every green tree; you shall tear down their altars, and dash in pieces their pillars, and burn their Asherim with fire; you shall hew down the graven images of their gods, and destroy their name out of that place. You shall not do so to the Lord your God. But you shall seek the place which the Lord your God will choose out of all your tribes to put his name and make his habitation there; thither you shall go, and thither you shall bring your burnt offerings and your sacrifices, your tithes and the offering that you present, your voice offerings, your freewill offerings, and the firstlings of your herd and of your flock.

(Deuteronomy 12:1—6)

The book of Job is read not only from the pulpit as part of the minister's message, but often as a form of public reading to civic clubs, social clubs, or study groups. It is a continuous dramatic poem. Is Job's faith in God strong enough, although evil befalls him, that he will still believe? This is the question which runs through the entire book. In preparing this selection for oral presentation, the reader should focus his attention on the theme itself and on its method of presentation. Three of Job's friends — Eliphas, Bildad, and Zopha, come to see him and thus follows the debate. Each speaks at length and in turn assails Job, and to each Job replies. There are three cycles of speeches. The oral reader must be aware of the three different visitors, emphasize the different speeches, and at the same time maintain the unity of the poem. He must also share with his listener the change in mood of Job at different parts of the poem. He is stung by the words of his friends from whom he expected comfort; he resents, as his speech shows, their implications of his wickedness. So must the reader reflect Job's total reaction and shifts of moods and attitude.

The answer of how to read is found in the literature itself, but one must study carefully and be sensitive to the emotion of the material.

Professor Grant in answering the question of how to read Job says: "As you would read one of the sublimest poems in the world, dealing with one of the most difficult problems that has ever confronted the human mind...It is one which every serious religious mind has to face sooner or later. Read it then first of all and until it becomes thoroughly familiar, as a work of art, not picking out a verse or chapter but as a whole."[6]

LANGUAGE AND STRUCTURE OF THE LITERATURE

Although it is necessary to know the background of a people to understand their literature, it is also useful to pay specific attention to the language itself, for it is through the language that thoughts and feelings are expressed. The Hebrews were a people of strong and vivid imagination. Since they dealt in sense impression and emotion, their language was primarily a language of the sense and emotion. The Hebrew poet depended upon the sound of language itself, and used language deliberately to create rhythmic melodic effects. This quality is illustrated in the following passage. Notice the rhythmic language and the melody of sound production. As stated before, no translation can reproduce the exact sound or emotion in the language of the original, but the translators were scholars of the Hebrew language and were aware of the use the Hebrew poet made of language to express his thoughts and feelings. Therefore, it is reasonable to believe that they would reflect the same in their translation.

> *"Who has measured the waters in the hollow of his hand*
> *and marked off the heavens with a span,*
> *enclosed the dust of the earth in a measure*
> *and weighed the mountains in scales and the hills in a balance?*
> *(Isaiah 40:12)*

A careful choice of words to create images to present thoughts and feelings is used frequently by the poet. The Song of Solomon also illustrates the use of sound rhythm and imagery. In this passage the imagery is strong and vivid.

[6]Grant, *op. cit.*, p. 68.

Hark, my beloved! Behold, he comes
  Leaping upon the mountains,
    Skipping upon the hills.
See, there he stands behind our wall.
  I look through the windows,
    I glance through the lattice.
My beloved spoke, and said to me,
  Rise up, my love,
    My fair one, and come away.
For, lo, the winter is past,
  The rain is over and gone;

The flowers appear on the earth,
  The time of singing is come,
    And the turtle dove's voice is heard.
The fig tree ripened her fruit,
  The vines are in blossom,
    They give forth their fragrance.
Rise up, my love,
  My fair one, and come away.

O my dove, that art in the clefts of the rock,
  In the covert of the steep place,
    Let me see thy countenance,
Let me hear thy voice,
  And thy countenance is comely.
                          (Song of Solomon 2:8–14)

Notice the musical words such as leaping, skipping. The description is vivid. "I glance through the lattice." "O my dove, that art in the clefts of the rock."

These literary elements are not an end within themselves, but they contribute to the total meaning of the scripture. The oral reader must be aware of the imagery and rhythm if he is to share with his listeners the high degree of emotion expressed in the poem.

Again we see the use of imagery and the simile, "be like a gazelle."

My beloved is mine and I am his.
  He pastures his flock among the lilies
Until the day breathes and the shadow flees.

Turn my beloved, be like a gazelle.
Or a young stag on rugged mountain.

(Song of Songs 2:16—17)

The oral reader must recognize that the use of the simile intensifies the imagery and contributes to the total poem. It is the task of the oral interpreter to determine how to approach the figures of speech in his presentation.

The prophet Jeremiah in telling of the wild northern hosts uses picturesque language and vivid images, for, as Julius Bewer said, "–He heard them coming, saw them galloping irresistibly onward over Palestine."[7] When he writes of this experience Jeremiah uses the visual and auditory images to share his feelings with all who will read.

My anguish, my anguish! I writhe in pain!
   Oh the wall of my heart!
My heart is beating wildly;
   I cannot keep silent;
for I hear the sound of the trumpet,
   the alarm of war.
Disaster follows hard on disaster,
   the whole land is laid waste.
Suddenly my tents are destroyed,
   my curtains in a moment.
How long must I see the standard,
   and hear the sound of the trumpet?

(Jeremiah 4:19—21)

How can the oral reader communicate the experience that Jeremiah recorded unless he is aware of the language used by the author to present the thought, mood and feeling of the scripture?

Contrast the language of the above poems with the language found in Proverbs. The purpose of Proverbs is to teach; hence, the author or authors use simple, well-chosen words. Epigrams containing a touch of sarcasm are mingled with warm personal exhortation to present the counsel of the Book of Proverbs.

Every word of God is tried,
   A shield for them that take refuge in Him

[7]Bewer, *op. cit.,* p. 154.

And thou not to His Words lest he reprove thee and
*   Thou be found a liar.*

                                              (Proverbs 30:5)

Hear, O sons, a father's instructions,
*   and be attentive, that you may gain insight;*
for I give you good precepts;
*   do not forsake my teaching.*
When I was a son with my father,
*   tender, the only one in the sight of my mother,*
he taught me, and said to me,
*   "Let your heart hold fast my words;*
*   keep my commandments, and live;*
*   do not forget, and do not turn away*
*   from the words of my mouth.*
*   Get wisdom; get insight.*

Do not forsake her, and she will keep you;
*   love her, and she will guard you.*
The beginning of wisdom is this: Get wisdom,
*   and whatever you get, get insight.*
Praise her highly, and she will exalt you;
*   she will honor you if you embrace her.*
She will place on your head a fair garland;
*   She will bestow on you a beautiful crown."*

Hear, my son, and accept my words,
*   that the years of your life may be many.*
I have taught you the way of wisdom;
*   I have led you in the paths of uprightness.*
When you walk, your step will not be hampered;
*   and if you run, you will not stumble.*
Keep hold of instruction, do not let go;
*   guard her, for she is your life.*

                                              (Proverbs 4:1–13)

In the oral interpretation of the scriptures from Proverbs the reader will need to assume the role of the public speaker, and read in a direct animated conversational tone. A discussion of the role of the reader and further suggestions for presentation of the material will be given in Chapter Three.

The literature of the New Testament is different from the literature of the Old Testament. The New Testament is not a history of people, but a record of a movement. It touches on history but is primarily biography in four different forms. The Four Gospels are the biography of Jesus.

The New Testament is written simply and naturally in the spoken Greek of the first century. The writers' aims were not to produce literature but to reach their public and get results. Although the language will not be as poetic as that of the Old Testament, nevertheless the New Testament is a literary achievement. Professor Scott points out, intent as they were on presenting the truth, the authors expressed themselves unconsciously in great language. For a fuller understanding of the context presented in this work the reader in his preparation should give close attention to the language used to express them.[8]

Although the New Testament is different from the Old Testament, you can follow the same approach of study and analysis. When you read from any one of the books, you should know who wrote the book, and to whom it was written, for what purpose and in what situation.

In the study of the New Testament, the reader must remember the Gospels were a new form of literature developed by Christianity. The writers of the Gospels do not deal with abstractions but with concrete and pressing questions.

The three gospels of Matthew, Mark, and Luke are independent works, but they have a close relationship to each other. In each Gospel the message in intended for all mankind. Each writer is telling the same story with the same purpose. The chief difference is in the style of writing and the language — two elements which will be discussed later.

Professor Scott in his discussion of the Gospel of Luke, points out that at the time when Luke wrote, Christianity had become a worldwide movement; it had spread out gradually from its first center in Jerusalem to the great capital in the West. At this time a number of documents were current, each presenting some aspect of the life of Jesus. Luke brought them together and blended and molded them into a unified record. Luke, in addition to wanting to present a real biography, had a missionary purpose; he was anzious

[8]Scott, *op. cit.*, p. 36.

for his works to be accepted by the public outside the church. In his writing he chose to present Jesus as the friend of the poor and outcast.[9]

Although Romans is often considered a theological treatise, close examination reveals it too is a letter in which Paul explains his position and defends it by reasoning and argument. Often he was attempting to answer some report that had come to him which had caused anxiety; other messages gave encouragement and instruction to a new church. What were the problems in which Paul was involved at Corinth? The reader would want to know before he could read the Second Epistle to the Corinthians.

Letters are usually thrown away when once they have been read and answered; but it was realized from the first that Paul's letters were not ordinary letters. He tells us himself that this was admitted even by his opponents.

"For his letters, they say, are weighty and powerful, but his bodily presence is weak and his speech contemptible..."
(II Corinthians 10:10)

Like many other great teachers Paul was unable to do justice to himself in public address and was easily eclipsed by a brilliant speaker like Apollos. Perhaps this was one reason why he took special care with his letters, in which he knew that he could express his mind adequately in a manner that compelled men to listen. The letters were written with care; therefore, the reader must study with great care not only the message presented, but also the language the author used in presenting the message.

In referring to the letters of Paul, Professor Scott says, "Even in point of language, the great passages have evidently been composed with studied art." He further states that every word had been deliberately chosen, the cadence of each sentence has been molded, as in the work of a great poet, with a view to a given effect.[10]

This would imply to the discerning reader that he too must study the language and the cadence of the sentence in order to understand the content.

In ancient times, as now, it was a common device to issue an open letter, a tract or pamphlet intended for the world at large. But

[9]*Ibid*, p. 77.
[10]*Ibid*, p. 109.

whenever Paul wrote, he had some definite purpose in view. For example, I Thessalonians was written to a community which had been Christian for only a few months. Paul assures the converts that he still maintains his interest in them; he congratulates them on their steadfastness and urges them to go forward. He closes the book with a series of counsel.

If the oral reader is aware of this background material, he can better understand the tone and mood of the writing and can share the message with his audience.

Although Romans is understandably considered a theological treatise, close study reveals it, also, is a letter in which Paul in simple direct concrete language states his ideas and defends them logically.

> *"I beseech you therefore, brethren, by the mercies of God, that ye present your bodies a living sacrifice, holy, acceptable unto God, which is your reasonable service.*
>
> *"And be not conformed to this world: but be ye transformed by the renewing of your mind, that ye may prove what is that good, and acceptable, and perfect will of God.*
>
> *For I say, through the grace given unto me, to every man that is among you, not to think of himself more highly than he ought to think; but to think soberly, according as God hath dealt to every man the measure of faith.*
>
> *Bless them which persecute you: bless, and curse not. Rejoice with them that do rejoice, and weep with them that weep.*
>
> *Dearly beloved, avenge not yourselves, but rather give place unto wrath: for it is written, Vengeance is mine; I will repay, saith the Lord.*
>
> *Therefore if thine enemy hunger, feed him; if he thirst, give him drink: for in so doing thou shalt heap coals of fire on his head.*
>
> *Be not overcome of evil, but overcome evil with good.*

The discerning reader will note that the mood and tone of Romans are somewhat different from the mood and tone of other biblical letters. The reader will be aware of the steps in the organization, and sensitive to the reasoning offered by the author, and he will reflect this understanding in his presentation. There are different means to accomplish this end. Some of them will be discussed in Chapter Three, but too much emphasis cannot be given

to the fact that no line of demarcation exists between preparation
and presentation.

A thorough preparation is the major element of the total
presentation.

Examine the following scriptures and note the relationship
between your understanding of the material and your oral interpreting of the passages. In your study give close attention to the
choice of words and how they contribute to the meaning. What word
pictures are given and what impact do they add to the emotion of
the message?

And he said to them, "When you pray, say:
"Father, hallowed be thy name. Thy kingdom come. Give us each
day our daily bread, and forgive us our sins, for we ourselves
forgive every one who is indebted to us; and lead us not into
temptation.
(Luke 11:2–4)

Now as they went on their way, he entered a village; and a
woman named Martha received him into her house. And she had a
sister called Mary, who sat at the Lord's feet and listened to his
teaching. But Martha was distracted with much serving; and she
went to him and said, "Lord, do you not care that my sister has
left me to serve alone? Tell her then to help me." But the Lord
answered her, "Martha, Martha, you are anxious and troubled
about many things; one thing is needful. Mary has chosen the
good portion, which shall not be taken away from her."
(Luke 10:38–42)

For David says concerning him,
"I saw the Lord always before me,
for he is at my right hand that I may not be shaken;
therefore my heart was glad, and my tongue rejoiced;
moreover my flesh will dwell in hope.
For thou wilt not abandon my soul to Hades,
not let thy Holy One see corruption.
Thou has made known to me the ways of life;
Thou wilt make me full of gladness with thy presence.
(Acts 2:25–28)

Read the scriptures aloud several times and each time be sensitive to the tone and mood of the words in the selection. Note the first selection is an example of a prayer; it offers instruction on how to pray. The second selection relates an incident. The reader is introduced to two women, Mary and Martha. Through the conversation we learn of the attitude of each of the women and Jesus' answer to Martha. The third scripture is more subjective; David is describing what he saw and felt. What demands does such preparation make on the reader?

One of the most interesting and at the same time one of the most difficult books in the Bible to understand is the Book of Revelation. The author is John who had been exiled to the island of Patmos. He is writing to the churches in the region to give them encouragement. Thus he writes for the people. Not only does Revelations contain a valuable message, but it is considered by many biblical critics to be the best literature in the New Testament.[11]

John describes how, in a vision, he sees the throne of God, surrounded by the hosts of angels. In the hand of God is a sealed book, and it is given to Christ, who begins to break the seals. As each seal is broken, a calamity falls on the earth. When the last calamities have taken effect the end is come. The last two chapters describe the opening of an age —

Then I saw a new heaven and a new earth; for the first heaven and the first earth had passed away, and the sea was no more. And I saw the holy city, new Jerusalem, coming down out of heaven from God, prepared as a bride adorned for her husband; and I heard a great voice from the throne saying, "Behold, the dwelling of God is with men. He will dwell with them, and they shall be his people, and God himself will be with them; he will wipe away every tear from their eyes; and death shall be no more, neither shall there be mourning nor crying nor pain anymore, for the former things have passed away."

And he who sat upon the throne said, "Behold, I make all things new." Also he said, "Write this, for these words are trustworthy and true." And he said to me, "It is done! I am the Alpha and the Omega, the beginning and the end. To the thirsty I will give water without price from the fountain of the water of life."

(Revelation 21:1—6)

[11]Scott, *op. cit.,* p. 277.

> *Then he showed me the river of the water of life, bright as*
> *crystal, flowing from the throne of God and of the Lamb through*
> *the middle of the street of the city; also, on either side of the*
> *river, the tree of life with its twelve kinds of fruit, yeilding its*
> *fruit each month; and the leaves of the tree were for the healing*
> *of the nations. There shall no more be anything accursed, but the*
> *throne of God and of the Lamb shall be in it, and his servants*
> *shall worship him; they shall see his face, and his name shall be on*
> *their foreheads. And night shall be no more, they need no light of*
> *lamp or sun, for the Lord God will be their light, and they shall*
> *reign for ever and ever.*
>
> *(Revelation 22:1–5)*

How to read Revelation? The oral interpreter must first be aware of the imagery, the choice of words, and the rhythm. The entire selection is an image, but note a few of the vivid images:

"Coming down out of heaven to God."
"He will wipe away every tear from their eyes."
"He who sat upon the throne said."
"And night shall be no more."
"He showed me the river in the middle of the street of the City."

As you read aloud and study the above selection, notice how each image is a part of the rhythm and contributes to the total meaning of the scripture.

TYPES OF LITERATURE

In the approach to the study of the Bible as literature, an analysis of the language has been discussed. Examples of the effective use of language by the author have been given and suggestions of how the oral reader can make use of these in his preparation have been offered. Another aspect of literature of the Bible is the structure or the form of the writing. It also is a vital part of the total selection, for it is through the structure or form that the author molds his writing. In a sense it is the container for the content.

The Bible contains many different types of literature; there are various acceptable literary classifications, but for the purpose of this discussion the following will be used: informal prose, narrative prose and poetry. This statement does not mean to imply that the classification was used in original literature of the Bible. But as has been pointed out, we can assume the translators reflect the style and form of the original literature in expressing its meaning.

Informal Prose. Addresses and letters are the two most frequently used forms of informal prose used by biblical authors. When an address is delivered, we can assume an audience was present, and that the purpose of the writing was to persuade or to convince. The prophet was not only one who foresaw, but also one who taught. Thus the prophet Isaiah represented the religious life of his time. He like other prophets addressed the people. The reader in communicating Isaiah's message will assume the role of a public speaker, and read directly to his audience in a clear, animated, conversational manner.

Paul, in his appeal to Agrippa, was delivering an address. He began simply and quietly, told the story of his life, and then went gradually to a higher level of persuasion. Although it is dramatic in nature, it is an address.

There are many examples of letters in the Bible; some are very personal and others resemble religious treatises. The Epistle of James and the First Epistle of Peter are straightforward exhortations, and resemble the address.

The letters of Paul range from short personal letters to theological treatises. "They have a peculiar and distinct character often rising into eloquence," says Dr. S. S. Curry. [12]

Each selection of the Bible that might be included in the general informal prose classification should be studied in accordance with the steps of preparation which have been mentioned. But this form of prose requires, in addition, a careful study of conversation as the mode of presentation. This suggestions does not imply that the reader should use a dull monotonous voice in his delivery. Conversation can be animated and interesting. The nature of these forms of literature does suggest the importance of the content or the message. The other aspects of analysis that have been discussed in this chapter can serve as additional guides for the oral reader in his preparation and presentation.

The book of Proverbs has been discussed as a didactic literature. It, too, is a type of informal prose. For many readers this type of biblical literature is the easiest to communicate. But the oral reader

[12]Curry, *op. cit.,* p. 70.

must be careful not to read it in a manner so void of feeling that it loses its power to awaken interest within his hearers. Dr. Curry suggested several years ago to "read with impressive seriousness a deep realization of the truth."[13] Although a writer today might say, "Understand your material, be sincere and read in good conversational quality," the two suggestions are the same. There is one word of caution: You should not confuse reading didactic material with reading in a dogmatic or negative manner.

Narrative Prose. The storytellers of the Bible have been recognized by those of all ages, who time and time again have gone to them as models of the art of narration. They understood men and women of all sorts and in all conditions.

In preparing to read a biblical story, the reader must understand the literary elements involved in narration, such as character, setting and plot.

The Bible contains many narratives. The story of Abraham, ready to offer his son Isaac, is highly dramatic and very moving. One of the masterpieces of narrative writing is found in the book of Judges. The story of Samson is the story of a tragic hero. The life of Joseph is a very skillfully told narrative. According to Professor Trawick, Samuel is the finest narrative book in the Bible. The style of the book is simple; the narrative easy, unified, and progressive, incident following incident as a well-connected story. The details are always sufficient to make the pictures and incidents vivid, distinct, and realistic; yet they are never dry or cumbersome. But the chief glory of the book is its masterly characterization. Here are real men and women, heroic enough to have a godlike vision of truth and righteous behavior, yet true citizens of the earth, where there is nothing absolutely perfect.[14]

Saul is one of the great and ironic tragedies of all literature. According to Dr. Julius Bewer, Saul's ability as a leader was first shown when the Ammonites attacked Jabesh in Giliad. Saul rose to the occasion, and it was this act of inspired leadership that won him the kingship.[15]

In this dramatic narrative there are well-described characters, Nahash, the Ammonite, Saul, Jonathan, and the people. Each person

[13]*Ibid.*
[14]Trawick, *op. cit.*, p. 91-92.
[15]Bewer, *op. cit.*, p. 15.

is introduced with description or explanation — for example, "Now Saul was coming from the field behind the oxen."

Intense dialogue is an important part of the story. The demand of Nahash, the people's reply, and Saul's speeches all reflect a great variety of emotion. The transitions serve to build the story, pointing out the change of character, place, time, condition — for example:

"Saul chose three thousand men of Israel. . . ."
"And the Philistines mustered. . . ."
"So — all the people went to Gilead —"
"One day Jonathan the son of Saul said to the young man who bore his armor. . . ."

The transition prepares for the conclusion.

"So the people ransomed Jonathan that he did not die."

The complete story is a dramatic subject in the rise and the fall of the monarchy, with lessons to be drawn from the catastrophe. The passages given below contain these elements and illustrate the literary value of the narrative.

Then Nahash the Ammonite went up and besieged Jabeshgilead; and all the men of Jabesh said to Nahash, "Make a treaty with us, and we will serve you." But Nahash the Ammonite said to them, "On this condition I will make a treaty with you, that I gouge out all your right eyes, and thus put disgrace upon all Israel." The elders of Jabesh said to him, "Give us seven days respite that we may send messengers through all the territory of Israel. Then, if there is no one to save us, we will give ourselves up to you." When the messengers came to Gibeah of Saul, they reported the matter in the ears of the people; and all the people wept aloud.
Now Saul was coming from the field behind the oxen; and Saul said, "What ails the people, that they are weeping?" So they told him the tidings of the men of Jabesh. And the spirit of God came mightily upon Saul when he heard these words, and his anger was greatly kindled. He took a yoke of oxen and cut them in pieces and sent them throughout all the territory of Israel by the hand of messengers saying, "Whoever does not come out after Saul and Samuel, so shall it be done to his oxen!" Then the dread of the Lord fell upon the people, and they came out as one man....

And they said to the messengers who had come, "Thus shall you say to the men of Jabeshgilead: "Tomorrow, by the time the sun is hot, you shall have deliverance." When the messengers came and told the men of Jabesh, they were glad. Therefore the men of Jabesh said, "Tomorrow we will give ourselves up to you, and you may do to us whatever seems good to you." And on the morrow Saul put the people in three companies; and they came into the midst of the camp in the morning watch, and cut down the Ammonites until the heat of the day; and those who survived were scattered, so that no two of them were left together.
(I Samuel 11:1–11)

So all the people went to Gilgal, and there they made Saul king before the Lord in Gilgal. There they sacrificed peace offerings before the Lord, and there Saul and all the men of Israel rejoiced greatly.
(I Samuel 11:15)

Saul chose three thousand men of Israel; two thousand were with Saul in Michmash and the hill country of Bethel, and a thousand were with Jonathan in Gibeah of Benjamin; the rest of the people he sent home, every man to his tent. Jonathan defeated the garrison of the Philistines which was at Geba; and the Philistines heard of it. And Saul blew the trumpet throughout all the land, saying, "Let the Hebrews hear." And all Israel heard it said that Saul had defeated the garrison of the Philistines, and also that Israel had become odious to the Philistines....
And the Philistines mustered to fight with Israel, thirty thousand chariots, and six thousand horsemen, and troops like the sand on the seashore in multitudes;.... The men of Israel saw that they were in straits (for the people were hard pressed), the people hid themselves in caves and in holes and in rocks and in tombs and in cisterns, or crossed the fords of the Jordan to the land Gad and Gilead. Saul was still at Gilgal, and all the people followed him trembling.
(I Samuel 13:2–8)

One day Jonathan the son of Saul said to the young man who bore his armor, "Come, let us go over to the Philistine garrison on yonder side." But he did not tell his father....
(I Samuel 14:1)

And Jonathan said to the young man who bore his armor, "Come, let us go over to he garrison of these uncircumcised; it may be that the Lord will work for us; for nothing can hinder the Lord from saving by many or by few." And his armor-bearer said to him, "Do all that your mind inclines to; behold I am with you, as is your mind so is mine." Then said Jonathan, "Behold, we will cross over to the men, and we will show ourselves to them. If they say to us, 'Wait until we come to you,' then we will stand still in our place, and we will not go up to them. But if they say, 'Come up to us,' then we will go up; for the Lord has given them into our hand. And this shall be the sign to us." So both of them showed themselves to the garrison of the Philistines; and the Philistines said, "Look, Hebrews are coming out of the holes where they have hid themselves." And the men of the garrison hailed Jonathan and his armor-bearer, and said, "Come up to us, and we will show you a thing." And Jonathan climbed up on his hands and feet, and his armor-bearer after him. And they fell before Jonathan, and his armor-bearer killed them after him;....

(I Samuel 14:6—15)

And while Saul was talking to the priest, the tumult in the camp of the Philistines increased more and more; and Saul said to the priest, "Withdraw your hand." Then Saul and all the people who were with him rallied and went into the battle; and behold, every man's sword was against his fellow, and there was very great confusion...

(I Samuel 14:19—20)

So the Lord delivered Israel that day; and the battle passed beyond Bethaven.
And the men of Israel were distressed that day; for Saul laid on oath on the people, saying, "Cursed be the man who eats food until it is evening and I am avenged on my enemies." So none of the people tasted food. And all the people came into the forest, and there was honey on the ground.
And when the people entered the forest, behold the honey was dropping, but no man put his hand to his mouth; for the people feared the oath. But Jonathan had not heard his father charge the people with the oath, so he put forth the tip of the staff that was in his hand, and dipped it in the honeycomb, and put his hand to

his mouth; and his eyes became bright. Then one of the people said, "Your father strictly charged the people with an oath, saying, 'Cursed be the man who eats food this day.' " And the people were faint. Then Jonathan said, "My father has troubled the land; see how my eyes have become bright, because I tasted a little of this honey. How much better if the people had eaten freely today of the spoil of their enemies which they found; for now the slaughter among the Philistines has not been great. "...

(I Samuel 14:23–30)

Then Saul said to Jonathan, "Tell me what you have done." And Jonathan told him, "I tasted a little honey with the tip of the staff that was in my hand; here I am, I will die. And Saul said, "God do so to me and more also; you shall surely die, Jonathan." Then the people said to Saul, "Shall Jonathan die, who has wrought this great victory in Israel? Far from it! As the Lord lives, there shall not one hair of his head fall to the ground; for he has wrought with God this day." So the people ransomed Jonathan, that he did not die. Then Saul went up from pursuing the Philistines; and the Philistines went to their place.

(I Samuel 14:43–46)

How can the reader communicate this story to his listeners? He must first have in mind the events as each follows and builds; he must be aware of the changes and shifts in the mood and emotion. The oral reader must understand the conflict within the story. He should note that the clash of ideas, as well as the clash of characters, produce the conflict. If the reader is satisfied with his understanding of these two aspects, he would do well to ask himself the following question: "Do I understand each character, and why he does what he does? Do I understand the relationship of each event to the total story. What transitions are used? How does the story conclude?" The oral interpreter in his preparation must be aware of the focal points of meaning, and of the units which form the build and lead into the conclusion of the story.

When the reader is aware of the different elements within a narrative, he is further motivated to his second task — to share what he has learned. The interpreter can share these moods and emotions through the tone of his voice and total physical reaction. Because of its context and its quality of literature, the biblical story of Saul will challenge the best in any reader in his preparation and presentation.

Perhaps the best loved story in the Bible is the Book of Ruth. It tells of the loyalty of Ruth, the daughter-in-law of Naomi, her diligence and prudence and her great reward. After the death of her husband and her two sons in Moab, where the sons had married the Moabite wives Orpah and Ruth, Naomi decided to go back to her native town of Bethlehem in Judah. In spite of her remonstrances Ruth insisted on going with her, declaring in those beautiful words, "entreat me not to leave thee."

Mary Ellen Chase describes the Book of Ruth as "one of the most charming and graceful of short stories not only in ancient literature but of any time in any language, and it well deserves the high place accorded it by critics of various countries and ages."[16]

Doesn't a literary selection of this quality deserve the best preparation by the reader? It is not necessary to be a literary critic to analyze and understand the narrative, but a few fundamentals are essential for understanding and appreciation. The story is told by persons who are called narrators. It is told for all who will listen. The setting is first in Moab and later in Bethlehem, and as Bewer observes, "tells the Jewish small town existence, with attention to character as displayed in ordinary human concerns."[17]

Naomi, Ruth, and Boaz are the most important characters in the book. A narrator gives the description and relates the events. Strangely enough, although the name of the book is Ruth, Naomi is the central character and, therefore, demands special attention on the part of the reader.

"A sequence of events with characters enacting them is the heart of a narrative," states Grimes and Mattingly.[18] Therefore, in preparation of the selection, the reader should have clearly in mind the steps and sequence of the story as illustrated below.

Naomi and Ruth arrive in Bethlehem at the beginning of the barley harvest. Ruth goes to the fields to glean. Boaz sees her and invites her to glean only in his field.

Given order to be kind to her.

Ruth asks why he should be so kind to someone from another land.

[16]Mary Ellen Chase, *Life and Language in the Old Testament,* New York, W. W. Norton and Company, Inc., 1962, p. 232.

[17]Bewer, *op. cit.,* p. 313.

[18]Wilma G. Grimes and Alethea Smith Mattingly, *Interpretation: Writer Reader Audience,* San Francisco, Wadsworth Publishing Company, Inc., 1961, p. 173.

Boaz's reply: *"All that you have done for your mother-in-law since the death of your husband has been fully told me, and how you left your father and mother and your native land and came to a people that you did not know before."*

(Ruth 2:11)

Naomi is told of Ruth's meeting with Boaz.
The reaction of Naomi —
Boaz was her near kinsman; Naomi makes her plea.
Ruth goes to Boaz.
Boaz promises to marry her if a closer kinsman did not claim her.
Ruth returns loaded with gifts and tells the good news to Naomi.
Boaz took Ruth as his wife.
The people rejoice and celebrate.
Ruth's son was born; Naomi became his nurse.

The reader will need to be alert to the language, both realistic and figurative, used by the author. It is not necessary or even advisable to attempt to impersonate the characters. But as the reader shares with his listeners the total impact of the story, the interpreter can vitalize the conversation by suggesting the characters. A technique which may be used by the reader and is also the method used by some of the teachers in Oral Interpretation is to place the characters in the area of the audience. The reader can assign each character a general direction of address and use it each time the character speaks. This approach will aid the interpreter to visualize the scene — not on the platform with the reader, but out beyond the audience, and will clarify the scene, identify the characters, and intensify the action. However, the same end can be accomplished through voice and facial and bodily reaction without the "placement of character." It is the interpreter's task to maintain the total unity of the narrative. He must bring all the elements of the story together to a purposeful conclusion. Only by careful study of sequence of events and remembering the opening and closing situation will he be able to accomplish his task.

A good interpreter would not attempt to read a story of Henry James, James Joyce, Mark Twain, or any author, classical or contemporary without study and analysis. Does a narrative from the Bible deserve less? Is it any less a narrative because it is in the Bible?

Poetry. The Bible contains many different types of poetry: ancient songs, lyrics, odes, and dramatic monologues. The Book of Job, for example, is dramatic poetry.

Suggestions offered for oral reading are applicable to all the literature of the Bible. However, there are certain aspects of poetry that require special consideration. By its very nature, poetry is compact and concentrated. This quality calls for a special use of language by the poet and a keen awareness of language on the part of the interpreter. Poetry deals not only with ideas but with emotions. The emotions encompass a broad scope of human experience, including the beautiful, awesome, ugly, average, or the nondescript. The consideration given to the emotion of poetry does not de-emphasize the thought of the selection, rather it intensifies the idea.

Poetic elements often give emphasis to ideas being expressed. For example the use of figurative language is a part of the Twenty-Third Psalm. The oral reader must understand the idea, but he must also know the other elements used to intensify and clarify the thought. The thought and emotion of a poem are so blended that it is difficult to say where one ends and the other begins. In expressing a thought, emotion, or experience the poet reveals his attitude toward that which he has expressed. This is true in the Twenty-Third Psalm. David is offering his praise to God in an attitude of serenity.

Symbolic language is also frequently used to express tone. The reader must give close attention to the symbols used if he is to understand the total meaning and to communicate to his listeners. The tone is easily discovered in such dramatic poetry as Job or Paul's plea to King Agrippa, for in each selection the speaker is quickly identified, and he in turn clearly reveals his attitude. In the more lyrical, subjective poetry such as some of Psalms, or portions of Song of Solomon, the tone is so interwoven with other qualities of the selection that it is not easily noticed. However, by careful study the tone can be discovered. As pointed out by Armstrong and Brandes, tone is not delineated by any set of rules or a formula. Its appreciation defines careful reading, a keen sensitivity and an awareness of words, and word relationships.[19]

Tone is very important to the oral interpreter. For it is through this device that he can reveal shades of meaning in what he is reading by the tone of his voice.

[19]Armstrong and Brandes, *op. cit.,* p. 256.

The reader could reveal much of the tone of this poem through his facial reaction and the way in which he focuses his eye contact.

The oral interpreter must recreate the images of the poetry, for it is through images that the poet intensifies and unifies the emotion and thought. The image may stimulate the reader's sense, but its effectiveness is in the reader's response. Therefore, the oral interpreter must present effectively the image in such a way as to elicit the desired response from his listeners.

Reference has been made to the use of figurative language. Examples have been given of the use of metaphor and simile. The oral reader must recognize the figure of speech, determine its purpose and relate it to the total meaning. Through the use of voice and physical reaction, he must point up this meaning to his audience.

A poet's ear is attuned to the sound of word, and therefore the oral interpreter must have a sensitive ear to the sound of poetry. The musical quality of sound is very strong in poetry. And although it can be appreciated for its own sake, sound may also reinforce or intensify the meaning. Because of the importance of sound, most poetry should be read aloud to be fully appreciated. This necessitates that the oral reader be aware of his voice with all its weaknesses and all its potentialities. For it is through the voice that the interpreter can share poetry with his audience.

In preparation for reading the poetry of the Bible, the interpreter should unify the thought or idea of the selection with the elements of poetry — emotion, figurative language, imagery, and thythm. For the oral interpreter must maintain the unity of the selection and at the same time point up the variety within the poem. Nowhere can greater variety in combination of rhythm and melody be observed than in the reading of the Bible.

Suggestions have been given on methods of analyzing biblical literature. In the discussion, the various elements of literature have been given as a part of the analysis. Understanding of the selection through analysis has been emphasized; however, no one would maintain that literary analysis is the answer for complete understanding of biblical literature. The suggestions given for the study and analysis of the Bible are offered to help the reader gain insight into the real purpose of the Bible. Is poetry less poetry because it is in the Bible?

Psalms. Perhaps the most revered and the most loved of all the biblical poetry are the Psalms. Mary Ellen Chase refers to the Psalms as one of the richest collections of poetry in any language because every emotion is within them.[20] Kenyon says the language of the Psalms has entered into our bones and colored our daily speech and literature.[21] The Psalms have been referred to by many authors as a high mark of religious poetry. Therefore the Psalms will be used for the basis of comments on understanding poetry.

Although it would be difficult to state how many were written by David, it is accepted by most of the Bible scholars that David was the author of many; therefore, let us assume David is speaking. He is recording and speaking for the Hebrew people. The book of Psalms contains expressions of progress, hopes, aspirations, and thanksgivings that are common to all humanity. In the 23 Psalm David is speaking in lofty praise and exaltation.

> *The Lord is my shepherd; I shall not want,*
> *He maketh me to lie down in green pastures: he leadeth me*
> *beside the still waters.*
> *He restoreth my sout: he leadeth me in the paths of righteousness*
> *for his name's sake.*
> *Yea, though I walk through the valley of the shadow of death, I*
> *will fear no evil: for thou art with me; thy rod and thy staff*
> *they comfort me.*
> *Thou preparest a table before me in the presence of mine*
> *enemies: thous anointest my head with oil; my cup runneth*
> *over.*
> *Surely goodness and mercy shall follow me all the days of my*
> *life; and I will dwell in the house of the Lord for ever.*
> *(Psalm 23—KJV)*

Psalm 122, generally attributed to David, is the song of the exiles when they set out on their march. It is a song of joy expressing their happiness that they had received a summons to go to the temple.

> *I was glad when they said to me,*
> *"Let us go to the house of the Lord!"*
> *Our feet have been standing*
> *Within your gates, O Jerusalem!*

[20]Chase, *op. cit.,* p. 227.
[21]Kenyon, *op. cit.,* p. 40.

Jerusalem, built as a city
*   which is bound firmly together,*
to which the tribes go up,
*   the tribes of the Lord,*
as was decreed for Israel,
*   to give thanks to the name of the Lord.*
There thrones for judgment were set,
*   the thrones of the house of David.*

Pray for the peace of Jerusalem!
*   "May they prosper who love you!*
Peace be within your walls,
*   and security within your towers!"*
For my brethren and companions' sake
*   I will say, "Peace be within you!"*
For the sake of the house of the Lord our God,
*   I will seek your good.*

                        (Psalm 122)

When the reader knows the setting and the purpose of the poem, he has understanding of the mood and feeling expressed in the Psalm. For example, in the following poem, Psalm 30, a very different mood is expressed from the one found in Psalm 122. The reader will note Psalm 130 is not a song of joy but the cry of the human soul and its longing for the forgiveness of God.

Out of the depth I cry to thee, O Lord!
*   Lord, hear my voice!*
Let thy ears be attentive
*   to the voice of my supplications!*

If thou, O Lord, shouldst mark iniquities,
*   Lord, who could stand?*
But there is forgiveness with thee,
*   that thou mayest be feared.*

I wait for the Lord, my soul waits,
*   and in his word I hope;*
my soul waits for the Lord
*   more than watchmen for the morning,*
more than watchmen for the morning.

O Israel, hope in the Lord!
For with the Lord there is steadfast love,
and with him is plenteous redemption.
And he will redeem Israel from all his iniquities.

The very popular Psalm 19:1–6 is an expression of praise of God's work in his creation. The people are speaking in the powerful beginning.

The heavens are telling the glory of God;
and the firmament proclaims his handiwork.
Day to day pours forth speech,
and night to night declares knowledge.
There is no speech, nor are there words;
their voice is not heard;
yet their voice goies out through all the earth,
and their words to the end of the worlds.

In them he has set a tent for the sun,
which comes forth like a bridegroom leaving his chamber,
and like a strong man runs its course with joy.
Its rising is from the end of the heavens,
and its circuit to the end of them;
and there is nothing hid from its heat.

To whom are they speaking? To all mankind? To all ages? How are they spspeaking? In a mood of exalted praise they are telling of the glory and power of God.

The public worship services provided opportunities for the individual worshippers to pour forth their thanksgiving or their petition in the temple. It is believed by many that the poet David wrote the songs to be given in the temple. Psalm 66 is an example of a song of thanksgiving.

Make a joyful noise unto God, all the earth.
Sing homage, all the earth, to God,
Sing out the glory of his name, and celebrate his praises.
Say this to God: "How dread thy deeds are!
Thine enemies cower before thy power,
All the earth bows to thee, singing thy praise,
Singing praise to thy name."

Come and see what God has done,
How dread his deeds are among men.
He turns the sea to dry land,
Till men cross floods on foot.
So let us joy in him who rules for ever by his power,
Whose eyes survey the nations, till not a rebel dares to raise
his head.
Bless our God, O ye nations, sound his praise aloud,
Who keeps us safe in life, and never lets us come to grief.
For, though thou hast put us to the proof, O God,
Testing our mettle, like silver,
Though thou hast let us be captured, let us be heavily chained,
Let conquerors ride over us,
Though we had to pass through fire and water,
Yet thou hast granted us a rich relief,
Setting us free in liberty.

So I enter thy house with sacrifices,
To pay my vows to thee,
Vows poured out by my lips,
Vows uttered in my agony;
Fat beasts I will offer thee,
The odour of burning rams,
Bullocks and goats in sacrifice.

Come, all ye worshippers of God,
Hear what he did for me:
No sooner had I called to him than I was praising him for
answering me.
Had I been thinking secretly of sin,
The Lord would never have listened;
But God has listened indeed,
And to my prayer he has paid heed.
Blessed to God who has not checked my prayer to him,
Nor his own love to me.

Imagine a reader, although very sincere attempting to read this
poetic Psalm without any knowledge of the situation, purposes, or
the poetic elements involved in the poem.

The 23 Psalm is rich in the imagery and beauty of language, but
expresses only one emotion, the author's own trust in God. All of

the images used by the poet to express the emotion are familiar; a shepherd and his flock, green pastures, still water, a table at which one sits quietly and serenely without fear of even the valley of the shadow of death.

> *The Lord is my shepherd; I shall not want. He maketh me to lie down in green pastures: he leadeth me beside the still waters.*
> *He restoreth my soul: he leadeth me in the paths of righteousness for his name's sake.*
> *Yea, though I walk through the valley of the shadow of death,*
> *I will fear no evil: for thou art with me; thy rod and thy staff they comfort me.*
> *Thou preparest a table before me in the presence of mine enemies: thou annointest my head with oil; my cup runneth over.*
> *Surely goodness and mercy shall follow me all the days of my life; and I will dwell in the house of the Lord for ever.*
>   *(Psalm 23)*

The approach which has been discussed is a way of getting at the sound, feeling, thoughts and language, or in short, the total poem. All of these elements areinvolved in the process of the creation of poetry. No serious student of biblical literature can afford to be ignorant of at least the basic elements of poetry. For as Curry said, "Does a lyric cease to be a lyric because it is in the Bible?" [22]

In his preparation for oral reading of biblical poetry, the reader should follow each phase of his study with awareness of the different elements of poetry. The reader must be cautioned not to emphasize any one element to the neglect of another. For example, it is easy to over-stress the rhythm of a poem, and neglect the imagery. Often the reader in his earnestness to read out the idea will neglect the tone and imagery and will lessen the impact of the thought. The interpreter must remember he is reading poetry, and poetry is composed of theme, language, and form.

The oral interpreter must also avoid two rather common problems in the reading of the Bible. Often the reader (in his eagerness) to present the dominant thought reads the Bible in a straightforward manner as if he were reading purely informative material. This type of reading neglects large portions of the total poem, and thereby

[22]Curry, *op. cit.*

distorts the total meaning. Other readers in order to avoid this mistake read the poetry in a sing-song manner. Actually many modes of presentation are available to the perceptive reader. If the interpreter concentrates upon the total poem, a sensitive, perceptive reading usually results. Sometimes, however, the interpreter reads each line as if it were a separate unit. This can result in choppy rhythm and a general lack of meaning. The reader must keep in mind that an end of a line in a poem is not necessarily the end of the phrase, clause, or sentence. The line in a poem must be considered as it is related to the other elements. It is not necessary to drop one's voice at the end of a line, but the reader may wish to recognize the line of poetry, and at the same time suggest when it is appropriate that the rest of the thought and feeling are to come. This can be done by the reader's holding on slightly to the word at the end of the line as he continues with the thought. This procedure will keep the rhythmical flow of the line and maintain the overall rhythmical flow of the poem.

"The oral interpreter should always be aware of the different elements of the poem as he studies and explores the selection, responding to the discovery he makes." [23]

Summary

In this discussion of the preparation of the oral reading of the Bible, it has been suggested that the reader study the historical background of the Bible, read different translations of scriptures, and consult the scholarly and critic writers of the Bible. It has been emphasized that the Bible itslef is the most important source of study. To understand the literature of the Bible, the reader should know who is speaking, to whom he is speaking, under what circumstances, and what he is saying. It will add further to the understanding of the Bible if the reader knows the style and structure of the material. The reader should study carefully the language of the scriptures, for it is through the language that the message is given. When these steps have been completed, the reader can further his understanding in reading the selection by making use of this additional knowledge.

[23]Armstrong and Brandes, *op. cit.,* p. 284.

Chapter Three
PREPARATION FOR PRESENTATION

In the preceding chapter attention was focused on the importance of a thorough knowledge of the material. This approach is basic to all interpretation, but is not enough within itself. The reader must have the skill to communicate his understanding to his listeners. And just as analysis of the material requires study, so does the art of oral reading require a skill. A skill based upon knowledge and practice. The oral reader should keep in mind the study and analysis he has made of the biblical literature. His study should form the foundation for his practice, and he must practice.

Readers Use of Voice

Body and voice are two-fold instruments for the oral reader. He learns to control them and to use them unobtrusively. The body, through posture and bodily reaction makes its contribution to communication. But it is the voice which is basic to oral reading. In oral interpretation the voice should never call attention to itself; however, development of the voice does require understanding and control. The reading of literature often requires more control and more flexibility in voice than is required in the average informal daily conversation. A good voice is one which is easily understood and pleasant to listen to.

PROJECTION
A good voice must be clearly heard, for a reading which cannot be heard is of little value. However, the interpreter should not confuse projection with loudness. Often when one is told to project, he gets louder. It is possible through the use of resonance and proper emphasis to project a whisper in rather low volume. A very quiet mood expressed in poetry may be communicated with little volume.

A voice that is too loud can detract from the reading. Imagine Ruth's answer to Naomi: "ENTREAT ME NOT TO LEAVE THEE" in a loud, shouting voice. Such a tone would destroy the meaning. The reader can sustain his voice but not resort to loudness. In reading the following scripture a quiet projection is required. The reader will need to be heard by all members of the audience in all parts of the room. This may require practice and reading of the verse several times.

> *Then Jesus went with them to a place called Gethsemane, and he said to his disciples, "Sit here, while I go yonder and pray." And taking with him Peter and the two sons of Zebedee, he began to be sorrowful and troubled. Then he said to them, "My soul is very sorrowful, even to death; remain here, and watch with me." And going a little farther he fell on his face and prayed, "My father, if it be possible, let this cup pass from me nevertheless, not as I will, but as thou wilt." And he came to the disciples and found them sleeping; and he said to Peter, "So, could you not watch with me one hour? Watch and pray that you may not enter into temptation; the spirit indeed is willing, but the flesh is weak." Again, for the second time, he went away and prayed, "My father, if this cannot pass unless I drink it, thy will be done." And again he came and found them sleeping, for their eyes were heavy. So leaving them again, he went away and prayed for the third time, saying the same words. Then he came to the disciples and said to them, "Are you still sleeping and taking your rest? Behold, the hour is at hand, and the Son of man is betrayed into the hands of sinners. Rise, let us be going; see, my betrayer is at hand."*

> *(Matthew 26:36—46)*

It has been emphasized throughout the text that the primary purpose of the oral reader is to communicate his material to the audience. If he cannot be heard, or if he is too loud, he has failed. To accomplish his purpose (as Lee states), "projection is the act of directing the voice to a specific target."[1] For the reader to accomplish this task, he must know the audience and the occasion, and adjust his projection to the particular situation. The minister, reading from the pulpit, often has the use of the microphone and, therefore, the projection is controlled mechanically. But the reader of the Bible

[1] Lee, *op. cit.*, p. 115.

should be able to read in the family circle, to a small group or in an auditorium and be able to gauge his voice properly.

Not only must the reader learn to project his voice effectively, but he must also vary the volume of his projection. The same volume, whether it be very loud or very soft, becomes very monotonous and meaningtess to the listener. However, a constant change of volume must also be interpreted as a lack of variety. The reader who is always changing the volume of his voice, and always modulating his voice may become very monotonous, for he is using variety for variety's sake. The reader uses variety in voice to achieve the emphasis and degree of audience attention he desires. Also, the mood of the selection calls for variety in the intensity of the voice.

The Book of Job provides an example of this need for a variation in the volume of the voice. Since the mood of Job changes several times, the volume of the reader's voice must vary to communicate the different degrees of intensity of feeling.

It is difficult to offer specific suggestions without appearing to be mechanical or dogmatic. There is no *one* way of making the projection of voice effective. The examples given are only to illustrate the importance of adequate projection, and they are to serve as guides, not as exact rules.

TEMPO

Variety in tempo is just as essential for effective reading as variety in volume. But it too must not be an end within itself. Variety of tempo for the sake of variety, or to show great artistry of the voice, can be as bad as no variety at all. The selection itself must determine the degree of variety of tempo. It is obvious that the following selection requires varying tempos. The selection opens with the statement, "And Jesus entered and passed through Jericho."

There is no one tempo that must be used, but the nature of the sentence suggests that a moderate tempo — not too fast or too slow — would be adequate. However, the situation and mood change in the following sentence, "And he ran before, and climbed up into a sycamore tree to see him." Therefore, the oral reader would need to adjust the tempo of his voice to the change of the mood. Practice reading it and be sensitive to the different moods and feelings. Let the tempo of your voice reveal the varying moods.

And Jesus entered and passed through Jericho.
And behold, there was a man named Zacchaeus, which was the
chief among the publicans, and he was rich.
And he sought to see Jesus who he was; and could not for the
press, because he was little of stature.
And he ran before, and climbed up into a sycamore tree to see
him: for he was to pass that way.
And when Jesus came to the place, he looked up, and saw him,
and said unto him, Zacchaeus, make haste, and come down, for
today I must abide at thy house.
And he made haste, and came down, and received him joyfully.
And when they saw it, they all murmured, saying, That he was
gone to be guest with a man that is a sinner.
And Zacchaeus stood, and said unto the Lord; Behold, Lord, the
half of my goods I give to the poor; and if I have taken any thing
from any man by false accusation, I restore him fourfold.
And Jesus said unto him, This day is salvation come to this house,
forsomuch as he also is a son of Abraham.
For the Son of Man is come to seek and to save that which was
lost.

(Luke 19:1–10)

The oral interpreter should practice reading at different tempos until he has developed a flexible voice, one that can respond and reflect the mood-intensity of the material. A change in tempo can gain the attention of the listeners and can intensify the feeling of the literature. In determining the tempo, the reader should review his analysis of the selection — who is expressing what thought, and in what mood. Read the selection and listen to your voice carefully and ask yourself whether the tempo communicates the mood.

The tempo of a person's speech is a product of his personality, his total background; and it is probably sufficient for his daily conversation. Often when it is suggested to an individual that his rate is too fast or too slow, his quick reply is — "It is my natural speed." Perhaps it is an habitual rate, and all the variety of range in speeds of the individual have not been developed. Therefore, the oral interpreter may need to adjust his habitual speech to communicate the thought and mood which is the message of his selection.

PAUSE

The use of the pause is one of the most effective of all devices to achieve good tempo. For the purpose of this discussion we will define the pause as *thoughtful silence*. The definition does not mean just a stoppage in speech, but it implies a silence giving time for the reader to think, reflect, or contemplate, and for the audience to think, consider, and react. Pauses provide the reader with a means of emphasis, a kind of oral punctuation, pointing up the significant, thoughtful and meaningful. Effective use of the pause can help set the tempo for the interpreter. Often the reader has a tendency to read too fast. In this case the pause can provide a variety in tempo that is sometimes difficult to achieve. However, it must be remembered that although the pause is effective, it can also be destructive. A misplaced pause or a pause that is so long that it gives the impression of strain can detract from the meaning. Read the following scriptures and give special attention to the use of the pause.

> *Give ear to my words, O Lord;*
> *give heed to my groaning.*
> *Harken to the sound of my cry,*
> *my King and my God,*
> *for to thee do I pray.*
> *O Lord, in the morning thou dost hear my voice;*
> *in the morning I prepare a sacrifice for thee, and watch.*
>   *(Psalm 5:1—3)*

Compare the different mood expressed in the following scripture to the feeling found in Psalms 5:1—3. How can you make use of pause and variety of tempo to communicate the mood of the selection effectively?

> *And men shall enter the caves of the rocks*
> *and the holes of the ground,*
> *from before the terror of the Lord,*
> *and from the glory of his majesty,*
> *when he rises to terrify the earth.*
>
> *In that day men will cast forth*
> *their idols of silver and their idols of gold,*
> *which they made for themselves to worship,*

to the moles and to the bats,
to enter the caverns of the rocks
and the clefts of the cliffs,
from before the terror of the Lord,
and from the glory of his majesty,
When he rises to terrify the earth.
Turn away from any in whose nostrils is breath, in of what
account is he?

(Isaiah 2:19—22)

The Beatitudes are particularly challenging for the reader because the repetition of the word *blessed* must be properly emphasized and at the same time not be permitted to become monotonous. Read the following scriptures aloud using pause and varying tempo in ways that seem to make the most satisfactory sense.

Seeing the crowds, he went up on the mountain, and when he sat down his disciples came to him.
And he opened his mouth and taught them saying:
"Blessed are the poor in spirit, for theirs is the kingdom of heaven.
"Blessed are those who mourn, for they shall be comforted.
"Blessed are the meek, for they shall inherit the earth.
"Blessed are those who hunger and thirst for righteousness, for they shall be satisfied.
"Blessed are the merciful, for they shall obtain mercy.
"Blessed are the pure in heart, for they shall see God.
"Blessed are the peacemakers, for they shall be called sons of God.

(Matthew 5:1—9)

Now read them aloud again. Note that you do not have to pause, or change tempo of voice each time you say the word *blessed* to express the meaning. For example you can shift the pause from the word blessed in the fourth line, to the word *meek* and at the same time achieve effective interpretation. This procedure is offered only as a suggestion to illustrate the use of the pause, and is in no way intended as a rule.

PITCH

The oral reader must be aware of the pitch of his voice. For the reader who can use various pitch levels is able to express shades and subtleties of meaning much more effectively than the one who cannot. Variety in pitch is as important as variety in tempo and volume. The interpreter uses pitch to clarify the meaning, to convey emotional state, and to emphasize a thought. The reader must be careful that he is not developing a pitch pattern. One can have variety in pitch and at the same time have a pattern. Thereader must let his voice respond to the mood. It is easy for one to develop a pitch pattern and difficult to correct it. One suggestion is offered — practice reading a selection with different emphases and mark off different pitches.

The following selection offers a challenge to the oral interpreter to vary the pitch level in accordance with the thought and mood. The language used is very simple, but the meaning expressed is profound.

In the beginning God created the heavens and the earth. The earth was without form and void, and darkness was upon the face of the deep; and the spirit of God was moving over the face of the waters.

And God said, "Let there be light"; and there was light. And God saw that the light was good; and God separated the light from the darkness. God called the light Day and the darkness he called Night. And there was evening and there was morning, one day.
(Genesis 1:1—5)

For everything there is a season, and a time for every matter under heaven:
a time to be born, and a time to die;
a time to plant, and a time to pluck up what is planted;
a time to kill, and a time to heal;
a time to break down, and a time to build up;
a time to weep, and a time to laugh;
a time to mourn and a time to dance;
a time to cast away stones, and a time to gather stones together;
a time to embrace, and a time to refrain from embracing;
a time to seek, and a time to lose;
a time to keep, and a time to cast away;

a time to rend, and a time to sew;
a time to keep silence, and a time to speak;
a time to love, and a time to hate;
a time for war, and a time for peace.

(Ecclesiastes 3:1—8)

This selection presents the problem of repetition very much as exemplified in the Beatitudes. It is also often read in the same manner and therefore becomes very monotonous. But the reader can practice reading the verses using different pitch on the word *time.* The reader may also vary the tempo and make use of pauses at the proper place and present a very thoughtful message in an effective way.

QUALITY

Quality has been defined as that component of voice not included in the other elements of projection, tempo, and pitch. It is frequently identified with personality. The voice is very responsive to the emotional condition of the individual. Therefore, the oral interpreter relies upon change in voice quality to convey the mood of the selection. The reader must be aware of any defects in his own voice that will call attention to himself and give his listeners unpleasant and undesirable reactions. Most voice quality defects can be eliminated by intelligent use of the vocal mechanism. Vocal quality is closely associated with resonance. Harshness, a common quality defect can be corrected or at least minimized by learning to relax the throat, and to improve vowel quality. Nasality can be minimized in the same way. It is accepted that some nasality is helpful to resonance, but an excess of nasality is a detriment to oral reading. Sometimes a breathy voice is substituted for a soft one. One way to eliminate breathiness is to learn to control the breathing mechanism.

The emphasis on the voice and suggestions offered for correcting and developing it do not imply that the oral interpreter should strive for a "beautiful" or "elegant" voice. The reader's voice should not call attention to itself. His voice, enunciation, and resonance are unpretentious and unobtrusive. The aim of the reader of the Bible is not to be a polished performer but to have the Scriptures heard and understood. In order to do this he should examine his voice. Is it free from any defects which will distract from his reading?

Good speech must be easily heard and pleasant to listen to. It must not only be audible, it must be articulate. The oral interpreter will want to be aware of his use of speech sounds. He will want them to be distinct, and correct. The reader cannot expect his audience to give their attention to the selection if they cannot understand the speech sounds. To develop accuracy in producing speech sounds, the reader will be sensitive to the vowel sounds. As the vowel is somewhat a musical sound, the reader will want to give it adequate amplification to produce the tone quality. The consonant sounds, when pronounced correctly, add much to the distinctness of speech.

In the following selections the reader should be aware of the tone quality inherent within the language. Special attention should be given to the sounds that produce tone and distinctiveness. For example, the vowel sound found in *you* and *your* and the repetition of the word. In contrast note the use of vowel in *not, iota,* and *dot.*

"Blessed are you when men revile you and persecute you and utter all kinds of evil against you falsely on my account."
Rejoice and be glad, for your reward is great in heaven, for so men persecuted the prophets who were before you.
(Matthew 5:11–12)

For truly, I say to you, till heaven and earth pass away, not an iota, not a dot, will pass from the law until all is accomplished.
(Matthew 5:18)

"You have heard that it was said to the men of old, 'You shall not kill; and whoever kills shall be liable to judgment.' "
(Matthew 5:21)

"The word which Isaiah the son of Amos saw concerning Judah and Jerusalem
It shall come to pass in the latter days
*   that the mountain of the house of the Lord*
shall be established as the highest of the mountains,
*   and shall be raised above the hills;*
and all the nations shall flow to it,
*   and many peoples shall come, and say:*

"Come, let us go up to the mountain of the Lord,
 to the house of the God of Jacob;
that he may teach us his ways
 and that we may walk in his paths."
For out of Zion shall go forth the law,
 and the word of the Lord from Jerusalem.
He shall judge between the nations,
 and shall decide for many peoples;
and they shall beat their swords into plowshares,
 and their spears into pruning hooks;
nation shall not lift up sword against nation,
 neither shall they learn war anymore.
(Isaiah 2:1—4)

If the reader in his eagerness to be correct is overprecise in his speech, it will detract from the material which he is reading. An over-mellow voice, or exactly clipped consonants will sound artificial, and become annoying to an audience. The voice is an instrument ot be used by the reader to convey the total meaning from the printed page to his listener. There are many suggestions that can be made for improving the voice. The reader can do much to improve his own reading by learning to listen carefully to his own voice. The use of the tape recorder is perhaps the best source for the reader. It can be a wonderful teacher. You should be able to control and use your voice adequately but always in an unobtrusive manner. The message is the important aspect; the voice only an instrument to convey the message.

Readers Use of Body

Bodily movement is governed by the general philosophy that regulates the use of the voice. Any movement or gesture must be unobtrusive and subordinate to the total meaning of the selection. Although the voice is considered more basic to oral interpretation than bodily reaction, this reaction is still important to reading literature aloud. We consciously or unconsciously observe the manner in which the reader approaches the platform; we notice how he stands to face his audience. The audience is quick to react to the "platform presence" of the reader. The oral interpreter should give attention to his posture, for it expresses the mental attitude he has toward himself and his audience. This approach in turn sets up attitudes in his audience toward him. An audience is sensitive to the physical carriage of a reader. It will resent the reader who is careless or slothful in posture, and it will equally dislike one who appears too formal or too precise in attitude.

POSTURE

The oral reader should strive to develop casual posture — not too formal and not slouchy, but one that lets the audience feel confident in him and one in which he feels comfortable. Imagine striding to the platform to read Revelation or rushing up to read Psalm 23. If you have formed poor habits in posture, the task of changing to good ones will seem difficult, and good posture will, at first, feel unnatural. Even the best speakers or readers sometimes have habitual negative actions, such as keeping hands in pockets, removing glasses, or leaning slouchily on the platform. A reader may be successful in spite of such habits. But one should try to correct any habitual actions or mannerisms that would distract from his reading. No one would suggest sets of rules for posture. There is no one way for a reader to stand. The exact choice of stance is a personal one, governed only by the situation and by the good taste of the reader.

BODILY MOVEMENT

The question is often asked, would one use bodily movement or gestures in reading the Bible? Again there are no set rules. But there are two factors to consider. The first, and perhaps the more important one, is the reader himself. Each interpreter develops an individual style of reading. Personality is closely related to gestures and movement. An active, outgoing aggressive person may use more gestures than the quiet, reserved person. One person might interpret a selection with no gestures, and only slight movements and be effective — another might use many gestures in good taste. The second factor to consider is the material being read. Job is a dramatic poem. It contains many of the elements of a play. The hill outside the city serves as a stage; the storm with lightning and thunder provides the atmosphere, Job and his friends are the characters. In recreating and communicating this dramatic selection to an audience, the reader may use gestures, or a small covert action to intensify the meaning.

Below are two biblical selections which could call for some gestures, action, or movement. You may want to practice these trying different movements or actions. However, in body movements and gestures, the reader should remain unobtrusive and never call attention to himself. The interpreter should be able to get a concept of how he is reacting to the impact of the material. Read the following scriptures and note your own reaction. How much physical reaction was involved?

I took them up in my arms;
  but they did not know that I healed them.
I led them with cords of compassion,
  with bands of love,
and I became to them as one
  who eases the yoke on their jaws,
and I bent down to them and fed them.

They shall return to the land of Egypt,
  and Assyria shall be their king,
  because they have refused to return to me.
The sword shall rage against their cities,
  consume the bars of their gates,
  and devour them in their fortresses.
My people are bent on turning away from me;
  so they are appointed to the yoke,
  and none shall remove it.

How can I give you up, O Ephraim!
  How can I hand you over, O Israel!
How can I make you like Admah!
  My heart recoils within me,
  my compassion grows warm and tender.
I will not execute my fierce anger,
  I will not again destroy Ephraim;
for I am God and not man,
  the Holy One in your midst,
  and I will not come to destroy.

They shall go after the Lord,
   he will roar like a lion;
yea, he will roar,
   and his sons shall come trembling from the west;
they shall come trembling like birds from Egypt,
   and like doves from the land of Assyria;
And I will return them to their homes, says the Lord.
(Hosea 11:3—11)

What physical reaction or bodily action would you use to communicate the message of Luke.

When he was at the table with them, he took the bread and blessed, and broke it, and gave it to them. And their eyes were opened and they recognized him; and he vanished out of their sight. They said to each other, "Did not our hearts burn within us while he talked to us on the road, while he opened to us the scriptures?" And they rose that same hour and returned to Jerusalem; and they found the eleven gathered together and those who were with them, who said, "The Lord has risen indeed, and has appeared to Simon!"
(Luke 24:30—34)

The interpreter in using any physical action should give total bodily response. His whole body is a sounding board for what he is presenting. It is difficult to suggest how one can develop appropriate gestures and bodily movement, for movement must be unobtrusive and spontaneous. It may be helpful in practice for the oral reader to exaggerate in his gestures and movements. Then when he appears before the audience for the reading, he can subdue his animation. The important thing is that the reader must be physically responsive. However, we should remember that the use of bodily reaction is governed to a large extent by the nature of the material itself. Brock in offering suggestions for bodily action says, "All bodily action should be motivated by the reader's response to the selection. Action itself is communication through visible symbols."[2]

The reading of biblical literature rarely requires broad gesturing or large exciting movement by the reader. The reader must learn to

[2]Harold A. Brock, *Effective Oral Interpretation for Religious Leaders,* Englewood Cliffs, New Jersey, Prentice-Hall, Inc., 1964, p. 60.

rely on suggestion of movement and action, rather than literal portrayal of movement. The mood and degree of intensity of the selections will determine the amount of the physical response. For example, if you are reading Paul's plea to Agrippa, you could not share the mood of this dramatic experience in a slouchy posture, or even in an over-relaxed one. The intensity of the selection calls for manifestation of tenseness of the muscles which would be reflected in total physical response. The interpreter's whole body is a sounding board for what he is interpreting. However, actions often vary, for the way in which an individual responds is governed to an extent by his own personality.

Below are three selections which call for different degrees of physical response or muscular tone. Practice reading each aloud until you feel you are responding to the narration.

I cry to thee and thou dost not answer me;
   I stand, and thou dost not heed me.
Thou hast turned cruel to me;
   with the might of thy hand thou dost persecute me.
Thou liftest me up on the wind,
   thou makest me ride on it,
and thou tossest me about in the roar of the storm.
   Yes, I know that thou wilt bring me to death,
   and to the house appointed for all living.

"Yet does not one in heap of ruins stretch out his hand,
   and in his disaster cry for help?"
Did not I weep for him whose day was hard?
   Was not my soul grieved for the poor?
But when I looked for good, evil came;
   and when I waited for light, darkness came.

My heart is in turmoil, and is never still;
   days of affliction come to meet me.
I go about blackened, but not from the sun;
   I stand up in the assembly, and cry for help.
I am a brother of jackals,
   and a companion of ostriches.
My skin turns black and falls from me,
   and my bones burn with heat.

My lyre is turned to mourning,
and my pipe to the voice of those who weep.

(Job 30:20—31)

"Blessed are you when men hate you, and when they exclude you
and revile you, and cast out your name as evil, on account of the
Son of man! Rejoice in that day and leap for joy, for behold,
your reward is great in heaven; for so their fathers did to the
prophets.
"But woe to you that are rich, for you have received your
consolation.
"Woe to you that are full now, for you shall hunger.
"Woe to you that laugh now, for you shall mourn and weep.
"Woe to you, when all men speak well of you, for so their fathers
did to the false prophets.
"But I say to you that hear, Love your enemies, do good to those
who hate you, bless those who curse you, pray for those who
abuse you.

(Luke 5:20—28)

I lift up my eyes to the hills.
From whence does my help come?
My help comes from the Lord,
who made heaven and earth.

He will not let your foot be moved,
he who keeps you will not slumber.
Behold, he who keeps Israel
will neither slumber nor sleep.

The Lord is your keeper;
the Lord is your shade on your right hand.
The sun shall not smite you by day,
nor the moon by night.

The Lord will keep you from all evil;
he will keep your life.
The Lord will keep your going out and your coming in from this
time forth and for evermore.

(Psalm 121)

Again it is difficult to offer specific suggestions of how much physical response should be given, and impossible to say how it should be given in each of these selections. It seems sufficient to say that total bodily reaction is effective in sharing emotion and attitudes of literature. Often the slightest physical response such as a twist of the head, a shrug of the shoulder, a slight shift of posture can communicate a feeling more accurately than the word itself; for as Brock stated, "Action itself is communication through visible symbols."[3]

EYE CONTACT

The question is often asked, should the oral reader use direct eye contact, and if so, to what extent? There are no simple answers. There are several arguments advanced against eye contact in reading the Bible. One is that the nature of the message requires reverence; therefore, the eyes should be fixed on the page. Others suggest that keeping the eyes fixed on the page gives the reader more freedom in expression through voice and body. One of the strongest arguments advanced against eye contact is that it makes it difficult for the reader to maintain his place on the page.

Considering these observations you must first determine your primary purpose and how you can achieve the purpose. It is rather obvious that the purpose of any interpreter in reading the Bible is to communicate the message of the scriptures to his hearers. If this message can be communicated more effectively by use of eye contact, then the reader should use this method. It is the message of the Bible that is important, not the particular technique used in its communication. The reader should be responsive in voice and body, but he should also realize that his eyes are as much a part of his communicating as is his voice. The third contention offers a greater obstacle, but it can be overcome. You must *know* the selection. Suggestions for preparation and study of the material have been given in Chapter Two. The reader must not only be thoroughly familiar with his material, but he must know *how* it is arranged on the page. This implies the importance of using the same Bible or manuscript in study and practice as you do in your public reading. The pages from which you are reading should be so familiar that an occasional glance at the page is sufficient. It is not necessary for the reader to

[3]*Ibid.*, p. 62.

memorize the scriptures. But he must know the material and be *familiar* with its arrangement on the page.

If you have decided to try to maintain eye contact with your hearers, you need to determine if it is always to be a direct eye-to-eye situation. It is true that direct eye contact helps to establish rapport with an audience, and it is also true that most audiences, perhaps because of customs of many public speakers, prefer and expect eye-to-eye contact. As has been emphasized throughout the book, the thought and mood of the selection determine the answers to most of the questions. What is the message? Who is giving it? and to whom and for what purpose? When you have determined the answer to these questions, then you can know the answer to the question, "Where should I focus eye contact while reading?"

For example, if one has decided to read from Proverbs, he observes the directness of style through the use of eye contact. The author is teaching and counselling. To communicate such material as this, the reader needs to speak directly with his audience.

Hear, O sons, a father's instruction,
  and be attentive, that you may gain insight;
for I give you good precepts;
  do not forsake my teaching.
When I was a son with my father,
  tender, the only one in the sight of my mother,
he taught me, and said to me,
  "Let your heart hold fast my words;
  keep my commandments, and live;
do not forget, and do not turn away from the words of my
  mouth.
  Get wisdom; get insight.

Do not forsake her, and she will keep you;
  love her, and she will guard you.
The beginning of wisdom is this: Get wisdom,
  and whatever you get, get insight.
Prize her highly, and she will exalt you;
  she will honor you if you embrace her.
She will place on your head a fair garland;
  she will bestow on you a beautiful crown."

Hear, my son, and accept my words,
  that the years of your life may be many.
I have taught you the way of wisdom;
  I have led you in the paths of uprightness.
When you walk, your step will not be hampered;
  and if you run, you will not stumble.
Keep hold of instruction, do not let go;
  guard her, for she is your life.

                                        (Proverbs 4:1—13)

References have been made several times to Psalm 23. In studying this poem, you will realize that the speaker is offering exalted praise to God. To communicate this mood and attitude, you will not wish to use eye-to-eye contact, but will suggest the subjective lyric with a somewhat reflective look. Professors Aggertt and Bowen offer excellent suggestions for the reading of any subjective or lyric poetry:

"The Revelations of intimacy found in lyric poetry deserve the finest of oral treatment. They must be handled with delicacy, so avoid eye to eye relationship with specific listeners when reading them. Through effective visible communication and vocal projection, you can still achieve audience contact even without eye contact."[4]

In this situation the reader is aware of the audience and is communicating to them, but he does not have direct eye contact. In reading a biblical story, the reader will probably use various means of contact; sometimes direct eye contact with the audience, in other places a slight change to indicate conversation of characters, and in some portions such as descriptive passages which include imagery, he may avoid the eye-to-eye relationship.

It has been emphasized throughout the text that the message of the Bible is the important factor. Posture, action, movement, and eye contact are but means of helping to communicate this message.

---

[4]Otis J. Aggertt and Elbert R. Bowen, *Communicative Reading,* Second Edition, New York, The Macmillan Company, 1963, p. 47.

Formulating the Introduction

After the reader has given adequate study and practice to the material, he prepares for the actual presentation. The wise reader considers his introduction, conclusion, and use of his manuscript very carefully. It is only the poor or inexperienced interpreter who plunges into his reading and out again without preparing his audience. Except perhaps for the most informal audience, and unusual occasion, listeners do prefer introductory remarks. The thoughtful reader polarizes the interest of the audience and brings it to focus on the material. He also clarifies the theme and mood of the selection. In other words the reader tries to establish a common ground on which he and his audience can meet and share the literature of the Bible.

In the worship service the attention focus has been accomplished to some extent by the singing of a hymn, a special number by the choir, or by some other aspect of the service. But for the individual who is reading for another situation, a careful preparation will be necessary. A provocative question, a rhetorical question, a direct statement to the audience, and many other approaches may be used to gain and focus attention. Whatever approach is chosen must be in keeping with the occasion and consistent with the literature you are reading.

What then should the introduction include to prepare the listener to understand and appreciate the selection? Obviously in reading the Bible, the chapter and book from which the scriptures are taken should be given. Often to give the translation you are using is helpful. But additional remarks giving pertinent background material, identifying the character, places of selection, central theme and purpose of the material are equally important. In your preparation, you were aware of the time and purpose of Paul's letter to the Church of Corinth. In your introduction share this information with your listeners, and it will help them in their understanding. The introduction gives you an opportunity to meet your audience and let them know what you are going to do. It gives you the chance to create the mood and attitude for the reception of your message. The introduction should be given in a conversational, spontaneous manner, although you may have worked very carefully to select the right phrase or word. If you prefer to extemporize your introductory remarks, you should prepare sufficiently so that you can speak fluently and not grope for words. If you decide to read your introduction, you must interpret it in a meaningful and communicative manner.[5]

Use of Manuscript

Oral readers differ on the use of the reading stand. Some prefer to hold the book or the manuscript. Others feel more at ease using the stand. There is seldom a choice for the minister. He is in the pulpit when he is reading from the Bible and, therefore, makes use of the lectern. But for the person who is reading biblical literature to a club, class or civic group, a choice must be made. There are good reasons for either approach.

If you elect to use the reader's stand, you are free to make gestures, and you may feel a certain freedom that comes from not holding the material. You may become more relaxed by occasionally placing your hands on the stand. This does not mean that you should use it as a support, something to lean on, but rather as a tool or technique to help you to communicate the message. For other readers the stand is a great hindrance as it seems to get between them and the listener. The good reader will do well to learn both methods: the use of the stand, or hold the book in hand. If you are reading to a small group, or in the family circle, it would be better to hold the book. When you are reading to a large group, the use of the stand might be preferable. If you so use the stand, do not permit it to hide you from the audience. Your hearers must be able to see not only your face but your total bodily stance and response. If you choose to hold the book, you must learn to hold it low enough not to block your face, and yet not so low that you cannot have effective eye contact with your audience.

In interpreting secular literature, the reader often prepares a manuscript. But in the reading from the Bible, the presence of the Bible is to be desired. It will be a constant reminder to the audience that what you are reading comes from the Bible. Therefore, care must be taken in the choice of size of book. A small New Testament, or any pocket addition is very easy to carry in one's purse or pocket, but although it is very accessible, it is not a good choice to use in

[5]Armstrong and Brandes, *op. cit.*, Discussion and examples of introduction, p. 155-165.

public reading. It is too small and is usually printed in small print on very thin paper conditions which make successful oral reading difficult. An average size Bible with medium or large print and with not too thin paper will serve the reader much better for public reading.

The advice and suggestions on use of stand or book may seem unnecessary if the material has been well prepared, and if the reader has developed his skills in oral interpretation. However, on the other hand, lack of mastery of these techniques can detract from well-prepared and otherwise effective reading. As Brock emphasizes, "...however the fact remains that in many oral readings, either the copy or the way it is used detracts from the reading."[6]

The oral interpreter can enhance his reading if he can handle a book with ease and let it assist him in his communication. If he uses a reading stand, he will use one that will not interfere or get between him and his listeners. He considers these devices as he does all techniques as means to an end, not as ends within themselves.

Concluding the Reading

Concluding often presents a more difficult problem than preparing the introduction. For you, unlike the public speaker, cannot state "now in conclusion," and yet somehow you must let your audience know you are concluding. You can do this in your manner of reading. A change in tempo, use of pause, or variation of pitch will indicate that you are approaching the last of the selection. When you have finished the reading, do not detract from the meaning by rushing to your seat. Pause and give time for the audience to think on what has been read, and then go to your place.

Summary

It is suggested that the reader have a thorough knowledge of biblical literature. In Chapter Two a procedure of study was suggested along with an understanding and appreciation of the selection. The reader should examine and evaluate his own skills for

[6]Brock, *op. cit.*, p. 80.

oral presentation. Is his diction clear and distinct? Can he be easily heard and understood? Are his two mediums of expression — voice and body — in tune to respond to the understanding of biblical literature? The actual oral presentation has been considered: the formulation of an introduction, the use of the reading stand, and the use of the book, concluding the reading. Does the message of the Bible deserve anything less than the best preparation for its presentation?

The reading of the Bible, to the family circle, or to a small group in a club or class, or from the pulpit, is not an easy task, but it is a challenging and rewarding one.

Chapter Four

PROGRAMMING

In the field of oral interpretation there has been a search for a new approach to group reading of good literature. This does not mean that there is less interest in or emphasis upon the individual reader. But teachers are aware of a need for a method to make literature more attractive and meaningful to students. Several different mediums have been advanced, such as choral reading, staged reading (sometimes called chamber reading or theater reading), and lecture recital programs. These mediums of interpretation can be utilized in the reading of the Bible. The following suggestions are given to show how these forms of interpretative reading can be used in biblical reading.

Choral Reading

Perhaps one of the oldest forms of group oral reading is choral reading. It had its beginning with the Greek drama and has been used in different ways to the present time. One of the most obvious uses of choral reading is in responsive reading. A well-prepared minister or some other designated person can make the responsive reading a vital part of the worship service. The two-part or antiphonal reading is the simplest form of choral reading, but it can add a dramatic element to the responsive reading. The Sermon on the Mount could be adapted to this form of choral reading, or a solo reader could be combined with the second part form for the reading of the Beatitudes. For example, a solo reader could begin reading with the first verse — the other two groups alternating the remainder of the selection.

The Sermon on the Mount
(Matthew 5)

Solo: *And seeing the multitudes, he went up into a mountain; and when he was set, his disciples came unto him: And he opened his mouth, and taught them, saying,*

1st Group: *Blessed are the poor in spirit:*

2nd Group: *For theirs is the kingdom of heaven.*

1st Group: *Blessed are they that mourn:*

2nd Group: *For they shall be comforted.*

1st Group: *Blessed are the meek:*

2nd Group: *For they shall inherit the earth.*

1st Group: *Blessed are they which do hunger and thirst after righteousness:*

2nd Group: *For they shall be filled.*

1st Group: *Blessed are the merciful:*

2nd Group: *For they shall obtain mercy.*

1st Group: *Blessed are the pure in heart:*

2nd Group: *For they shall see God.*

1st Group: *Blessed are the peacemakers:*

2nd Group: *For they shall be called the children of God.*

1st Group: *Blessed are they which are persecuted for righteousness' sake:*

2nd Group: *For theirs is the kingdom of heaven.*

1st Group: *Blessed are ye, when men shall revile you, and persecute you, and shall say all manner of evil against you falsely, for my sake:*

2nd Group: *Rejoice, and be exceeding glad: For great is your reward in heaven: For so persecuted they the prophets which were before you.*

Choral reading is also very adaptable to Vesper services. A group of people formed into a speaking choir, reading from the Bible, can be most effective. The regular choir might want to substitute the reading of Psalms for one of the songs in regular service. The 90 Psalm would be appropriate and easily arranged for such an occasion. Thus, a combination of scripture and poetry can blend into a program for a special type of presentation.

With a little imagination and a great deal of preparation, the possibilities are unlimited in the use of choral reading in programming for the church. This kind of reading is especially interesting to young people. In addition to vitalizing the literature of the Bible to them, it offers training in the important art of reading aloud.

Theatre Reading

For the past several years there has been an accelerated interest in staged reading.[1] This style of oral interpretation offers many advantages. For example, it can be produced on a small stage or in a classroom with little or no properties by two or more readers.

In this type of reading it is the narrator who maintains the unity of the story and keeps it moving. Sometimes the narrative role is assumed by the other readers of the group, each one taking the narrative part leading to the next dialogue. In some selections, the role of the narrator is assumed by one of the characters within the story. The division of the material is not so important if this division is based on purpose, and if it holds the unity of the selection. It has become an accepted (but not essential) practice for the readers to sit in chairs or on stools for the presentation. One reader may take lines of several different characters, indicating exits and entrances by turning to one side or turning back to the audience. The director can, through a little creativeness and experimentation, find the best stage of arragement for each selection. He should keep in mind that his purpose is to present Bible narrative in a lively dramatic manner. The dramatic poem, Job, with cutting and arrangement would be excellent for staged reading.

As in all good oral interpretation, a successful staged reading is the result of careful selection and arrangement of material, an understanding of the material, and a group of readers who can communicate the literature to their listeners. In addition to being an interesting experience for the participants, staged reading is another means by which the literature of the Bible can be presented in a meaningful and dramatic manner.

---

[1] Armstrong and Brandes, *op. cit.*, Appendix A.

Lecture and Theme Program

The lecture recital built around a theme is a type of programming that can readily be adapted to the biblical literature. The following examples will illustrate the scope and possibilities.

The subject of *faith* as given in the Bible might be chosen as the theme for a presentation. The program is opened with one person reading from the 11th chapter of Hebrews. As the reader identifies an act of faith, another interpreter reads the story or a portion of the story that has been identified. As he finishes the story, the first reader picks up the narrative and continues until another character or act of faith is given. This procedure is followed with one reader serving as narrator, holding the unity and reading the transition between each story until the program is concluded. This same kind of program could be presented by one reader. Paul's letters can be arranged into a lecture form program. The group could have a general discussion of Paul, the early churches, and the setting and theme of letters. At an appropriate time within the discussion, another member, after a few introductory remarks, might read one of the letters. The theme will continue with discussion and reading.

In building and arranging the programs, care must be taken to observe a few general principles. Each selection should be placed so that it will receive the most favorable response from the audience. There are four major principles in arranging a sequence of material; opening selection, transition from one selection to another, the climatic selection, and the conclusion. The first selection should generally be brief; a narrative is a good choice to get the attention of the audience. In addition to a selection that will add variety and contrast in transitional material, the reader may add extemporaneous remarks between the selections. The material should be arranged in a manner that will build to a climax. There are no hard and fast rules to govern what selection should be placed at the climax. But the major selection is suggested as the climactic one, and should be placed near the close of the program. The concluding number should be short and should serve to unify the total program. It should give the listener a feeling that the reading is complete. The discussion should be well prepared and so outlined as to be an intricate part of the total program.

Summary

The suggestions on programming are rather general and are not intended to be comprehensive or dogmatic, but are offered only to show the possibilities of different mediums of interpretation and to illustrate methods of approach.

SUGGESTED READING

Aggertt, Otis J. and Elbert R. Bowen, *Communicative Reading,* 2nd Edition (New York: The MacMillan Company, 1963).

Armstrong, Chloe and Paul Brandes, *The Oral Interpretation of Literature* (New York: McGraw-Hill Book Company, 1963).

Bewer, Julius A., *The Literature of the Old Testament,* 3rd Edition, Rev. by Emil G. Kraeling (New York & London: Columbia University Press, 1962).

Brock, Harold A., *Effective Oral Interpretation for Religious Leaders* (Englewood Cliffs, New Jersey: Prentice-Hall, Inc., 1964).

Brooks, Cleanth and Robert Penn Warren, *Understanding Fiction,* 2nd Edition (New York: Appleton-Century-Crofts, Inc., 1959).

_____, *Understanding Poetry,* Rev. (New York: Holt, Rinehart, and Winston, Inc., 1950).

Chase, Mary Ellen, *The Bible and the Common Reader,* Rev. Edition (New York-Chicago: The MacMillan Company, 1963).

Chase, Mary Ellen, *Life and Language in the Old Testament* (New York: W. W. Norton and Company, Inc., 1962).

Curry, S. S., *Voice and Literary Interpretation of the Bible* (New York: George H. Doran Company, 1905).

Geiger, Don, *The Sound, Sense, and Performance of Literature,* (Chicago: Scott, Foresman and Company, 1963).

Grant, Frederick C., *How to read the Bible* (New York: Morehouse-Gorham Company, Collier Books, 1956).

Grimes, Wilma G. and Alethea Smith Mattingly, *Interpretation: Writer, Reader, Audience* (San Francisco: Wadsworth Publishing Company, Inc., 1961).

Hunter, A. M., *Interpreting the New Testament* (Westminster, 1952).

Kenyon, Sir Frederic, *The Reading of the Bible* (London: John Murray, Albermarle Street W., 1944-1945).

Lee, Charlotte I., *Oral Interpretation,* Second Edition (Boston: Houghton Mifflin Company, 1959).

Lantz, J. Edward, *Reading the Bible Aloud* (New York: The MacMillan Company, 1959).

Perrine, Lawrence, *Sound and Sense: An Introduction to Poetry* (New York: Harcourt, Brace, and Company, Inc., 1956).

Scott, Ernest Findlay, *The Literature of the New Testament* (New York: Columbia University Press, 1932).

Trawick, Buckner B., *The Bible As Literature* (New York: Barnes and Noble, Inc., 1963).